THE HOLOCAUST

THE HOLOCAUST

FROM A SURVIVOR OF VERDUN

William Hermanns

WITH DRAWINGS BY PAUL BACON

1817

HARPER & ROW, PUBLISHERS

NEW YORK, EVANSTON

SAN FRANCISCO

LONDON

To my sister Gretel, who during the holocaust of the Kaiser's World War dedicated herself to sending food parcels to the starving soldiers in the trenches of Russia and France yet was to perish during Hitler's holocaust in a concentration camp

CONTENTS

Verdun (vĕrdŭn', vàr'dun, Fr. vĕrdŭ'), town (pop. 18,000), Meuse dept., NE France, in Lorraine, on the Meuse river. Here 2,000,000 men were engaged in the longest and costliest battle of the First World War; 1,000,000 were killed. A determined German offensive, led by Crown Prince Frederick William, opened the battle on February 21, 1916. Vaux and Douaumont were taken but Verdun repulsed all assaults. Petain rallied the French resistance with the phrase, "They shall not pass." Although unsuccessful, a British offensive on the Somme relieved the immediate pressure on Verdun, and by December, 1916, the French had recovered most of the lost ground. In 1918 the Americans and French were victorious in the Verdun sector.

INTRODUCTION

Eben dasjenige, was niemand zugibt, niemand
hören will, muss desto öfter wiederholt werden.
　　　　　　　　　　　—GOETHE

　—What no one admits, what no one wants to hear, is precisely
　that which has to be repeated all the more.

In the spring of 1968 at San Jose State College in California, where I had taught for nineteen years before my retirement, I was confronted by a student delegation with the request to address an assembly of about 25,000 students striking in protest of the war in Vietnam. I was asked to read part of a manuscript written fifty years earlier, my recollections of the battle of Verdun, a manuscript which had been read by many of my students throughout the years and which they told me was being intensely discussed at the time. It was their feeling that what had happened at Verdun was again happening in Vietnam.

How a nation like Germany in 1914 or the United States in the 1960s could get itself into such a situation is a matter for historians to explore. My concern is with the people, young and old, soldiers and civilians, whose lives are permanently affected and often destroyed because of policy decisions and political expediency.

My involvement in World War I extended from May of 1915 to January of 1920. Of this time, I spent a year and more in the trenches of the Argonne Forest, two months in the sector of Verdun, and then forty months in French captivity, including a full year after the end of the war to rebuild the destroyed area around Verdun. From these almost five years in uniform, four days in the battle of Verdun had an effect on my future life that remains with me to this day. I first wrote of what I saw and felt immediately upon the first days of my captivity. These memories grew to a volume, which, under grave danger, I had to smuggle out of Germany, as the Nazi regime sent to concentration camp anyone who even mentioned the word "Verdun."

It is my hope that the story of what I saw and felt, recounted here, will help the cause of peace by illustrating its alternative —war. Whether the battlefield is France or Indochina, the harvest of death and horror is the same. It is my conviction that humanity deserves better.

THE HOLOCAUST

I. INITIATION TO MANHOOD

The war began for me as a religious crusade. The Kaiser declared, "The Russians, French, and English have united to destroy our sacred heritage; they are jealous of our accomplishments." I listened and faithfully agreed, for to me the Kaiser was God's emissary on earth.

What an awesome sight! Battalion after battalion marching past our house and garden toward the west. How eager the young men looked, as though they might encounter the enemy at the next corner. How handsome were their gray battle uniforms, with their spiked helmets adorned with German eagles! How tanned and grim the sun made their faces! And how proud they were of being worthy to carry rifles on their shoulders.

War had certainly become the German initiation to manhood. The songs of war were irresistible, sweeping, and threatening as they gushed from a thousand throats! *"Siegreich wollen wir Frankreich schlagen, sterben als ein tapferer Held."* ("Victoriously we will crush France and die as brave heroes.") Four abreast, in equal steps they marched by and vanished, leaving only the echo of their songs and boots behind.

1

On one of these hot August days, my guardian, Aunt Veronica, instructed the maids to place pails of water along the sidewalk and stand with coffee and cups. But this beneficence was little appreciated. A captain, sitting high on his horse, threatened the maids with his whip and ordered a soldier, who had stepped out to take a cup of coffee, to kick over the pails. My rotund little aunt, fierce but dignified, came out to face him. "You cannot march on like that," she said. I took the officer's side, saying for all to hear, "Discipline befits the hero." The captain gave a salute from his horse, his whole face gleaming. His big blond mustache seemed to become the Kaiser's very own when he said, "We need boys like you! Come and join." What glory it would be to volunteer!

Soon Liège fell. But even though my cousin George died in the conquest of this Belgian fortress, my yearning for the glory of battle was not dampened. During a visit of condolence to George's mother, Aunt Rosalia, I found her wrapped in black crêpe, walking from room to room, moaning, "If only he could come back, even without arms and legs! I would gladly carry him."

I quoted the inscription over the portal of my school, *"Dulce et decorum est pro patria mori."* ("It is sweet and seemly to die for your native land.") And was it wrong? The clergy blessed the weapons; the people stood behind the Kaiser; and even the Kaiser's despised foes, the Socialists, voted for the war budget and rallied around His Majesty, who announced, "I no longer recognize political parties, I only know Germans." And everyone went to war, spiritually if not physically. I, too. And why not? Down with the French, who had tried to export their ideas of revolution to us. Let them boast of the triumph of reason over exploitation and superstition. Down with the British and their Magna Carta, with their spineless pragmatism and their boast of human dignity. What sort of culture is this which erects scaffolds in London and Paris to behead their kings? We Germans can boast of something greater. We believe in order, and not revolution. We believe in obedience to those whom Providence has chosen to command, and not in an individualism that challenges the prerogatives of the State. So what if the world does take exception to our *Weltanschauung* imbued with militarism? Didn't Bismarck say, "Let them hate us as long as they fear us"? In the spirit of the Iron Chancellor, who once said that great decisions are not taken by referendums but by blood and iron, our chancellor, von Bethmann-Hollweg, had rebuked those who objected to the violation of our neutrality treaty with Belgium. He declared, "Treaties are scraps of paper."

My aunt had not wanted me to join, protesting, "Don't think war is a carnival. I have seen three wars: against Denmark, Austria, and France. I have seen the wounded and dying carried from the trains." But it was not she to whom I listened. I placed her in front of the portrait of my grandfather and said, "He was not a coward, and I am not a coward. My brother and six cousins have already joined. The Kaiser calls, and I will follow him. In four weeks, he will make his triumphant entrance through the Arc de Triomphe and I will march at his side." I read to her a passage from a newspaper in which the Kaiser stated in a speech, "Let them perish, all the enemies of the German people! God demands their destruction; God who through my mouth bids you to do His will." My aunt replied that this anointed of God once said to his soldiers who marched to China, "Give no quarter to prisoners. Act in China like Huns. For a period of a thousand years, no Chinese shall dare raise his eyes before a German!" I cautioned my aunt to tell this to no one, for she could have been arrested for treasonable propaganda. "Imagine," she cried, "no quarter to a helpless prisoner. Suppose you fall into the hands of a Frenchman or a Russian. I still believe in the scriptures: 'Do unto others as you would have others do unto you,' and, 'Who takes up the sword shall perish by the sword.'"

The next morning, I packed a small suitcase and left my aunt's home in Neuwerk. At the station of Neuss, where passengers changed trains for Cologne, I was joined by a friend, Peter Kamp. We viewed a seemingly endless military train pulling slowly out of the station. Pandemonium reigned, with mothers and sweethearts on the train's running boards embracing flower-covered soldiers. Photos of the Kaiser and his generals were plastered on the train. In huge chalk lettering under the posters was written, "*Jeder Schuss ein Russ; jeder Tritt ein Britt; jeder Stoss ein Franzos.*" ("For each bullet a Russian; for each kick an Englishman; for each shove a Frenchman.") After arriving in Cologne, we marched through the streets with hundreds of youngsters, sons of both the rich and the poor, arm in arm and fourteen abreast, singing as if in one voice, "*Deutschland über Alles.*" However, there were so many volunteers at the recruiting station that we were not accepted. "Let us hope we see action before the war is over," said Peter as we rode home together on the train.

Early the following morning, I was roused by a street noise and the knockings of maids as they ran from door to door awakening everyone. The dogs were barking and from the meadows came the mooing of cows. Was there a fire? What was the yelling about? "The French are coming!" What a scene— hundreds of people, mostly women, running in their wooden shoes toward the highway leading to Krefeld, brandishing pitchforks, knives, and hammers. They yelled at our maids, "Come along—defend our country." My aunt, ordering the maids back into the house, was stopped by the wife of our gardener, the mother of eight children, who, in her best attempt at High German, said to my aunt, "Miss Veronica, if we do not stop the French, they will massacre us like dogs, and our pigs, goats, and cattle they will take away." And then, from under her blue apron, she drew out a bread knife, shouting, "Mistress, with this knife I will stab the belly of the first Frenchman I meet!" My aunt stepped back, faced the woman with her fanatic eyes, and queried, "Margaret, isn't that the knife you cut bread with for your children?" My aunt returned to the house and spoke to me the words of Schiller, "And there the women have become hyenas."

A few days later, in Essen, I was to witness yet another emotion-laden scene: were it not for police protection, an elegantly dressed woman, having already been dragged for some considerable distance by a mob, would have been lynched in the street. People in the crowd cried out, "She is a French spy, she wears a wig, she is a man!" I ran with the crowd to witness the outcome. In front of the city hall where the accused was held, a chauffeured limousine suddenly arrived. Out of the car stepped Bertha Krupp, with her husband, von Bohlen, and a friend, to rescue the woman. The pseudo-French spy, who indeed wore a Parisian dress and a fitting hairdo, was identified as the wife of a director of the Krupp munitions plant.

Several months later, I was accepted into the army, grateful that the Kaiser's prediction that the war would be over by Christmas had not come true.

II. GODS IN UNIFORM

In the spring of 1915, I was dispatched with some hundred other "war eagerlings" by special train to the North German town of Salzuflen, to fill the depleted ranks of an *Ersatz-battalion*. When we arrived, we found the station charmingly decorated with pots of geranium and fuchsia. We were met by a staff-sergeant-lieutenant, a rank created during the war to honor meritorious staff sergeants who had many years of service with a lieutenant's high collar and epaulets, without allowing them, however, to eat in the officers' casino.

This officer marched us in files of four to our quarters, but without the air of those feared sergeants I had, as a child, so often seen in Koblenz who seemed to have been born wearing hobnailed boots for kicking the recruits around.

Our sergeant-lieutenant had smiling eyes and a finely groomed goatee, and he wore a peaked helmet on which a gold eagle glittered in the May sun. His field-gray uniform was so well fitted that it must have been tailor-made. A beautiful thing to wear a uniform, especially when one can climb, as I, a "one-year man," was privileged to do, up the echelon of the officer corps, without any social barriers.

I imagined coming home wearing the Iron Cross, and parading it before the eyes of my girl friend Toni, with whom I had read so many of the plays of Ibsen—and would still be her friend if it had not been for my own stupidity. I had invited my friend Meinhard to read a part in our play, and a long-lasting friendship among us three developed. Alas, her beautiful dark eyes looked to him more often than to me. I must admit he was a head taller than I, had blue eyes and blond hair, and was not as impetuous, but mature, gentle, and wise. Yet, with an Iron Cross, I looked forward to enticing Toni's eyes again. The hope of winning Toni was strengthened by her appearing on the platform at the Essen Station with Dora, another girl friend of mine. She held an onion in her hand while Dora had a bedsheet in which to cry. Each pretended to be overwhelmed by grief, weeping tears in the bedsheet. Capering about as they did, they soon succeeded in cheering me up, as well as the rest of the recruits in the compartment. The girls helped them forget their own sorrow and their mothers who wept in earnest.

I now wondered if my comrades before, behind, and beside me also thought of the Iron Cross. Most of them wore sweaters under their Sunday coats. All looked husky—probably men either accustomed to hard labor or from the country. We all carried a prescribed pack with our home addresses, and I'm sure each contained pieces of cake from our mothers. My Aunt Veronica had filled mine with a huge cake, cookies, and chocolate, telling me to share them, especially with my immediate superiors, such as the room head or the corporal. My aunt knew —she had lived through three wars and had learned from her brothers, cousins, and neighbors what sort of people a recruit meets in his platoon and company.

My reflections ceased, for our march had stopped. We had

reached an inn on the outskirts of Salzuflen, where about a
hundred men were to take quarters in a formal dance hall.
There were three tiers of beds, and immediately each of us was
given an unbleached sheet, a blue-and-white checkered pillow-
case, and two blankets. Under the supervision of a corporal, I
made my first bed.

No sooner was this done than the corporal had us line up,
two by two, asking, "Who among you are one-year men?" A
young man wearing gold-rimmed spectacles and I stepped forward.

"So you are the ones who went to privileged schools and only
have to serve one year, while we common people must stay two
or three. You will soon be officers, a rank I will never attain
even if I served twenty years. You will soon be able to have me
stand at attention at your will. . . . But we are not that far
along yet. Before you become officers, you must become men.
And I'm here to help you. You had governesses at home who
waited on you hand and foot. Now we shall make you men." He
gave each of us a small scrubbing brush, and, pointing to pails
near the entrance, said, "Each one of you take a pail, go to the
back yard, where you will find a faucet, fill them, and clean the
latrine." We went. I couldn't see why this duty would cause
such hilarity among the other men, yet when we passed the line
to the door, I saw everyone grinning.

Outside I had a chance to become acquainted with my companion. His name was Theodor Hilgers; he was a student of
theology, had a pockmarked face, and eyes that shone pale blue
behind his glasses. When we approached the latrine with full
pails, we stood transfixed. Had this small place served for the
whole regiment? To describe here the filth, the stench, and the
spit would make the paper blush. We worked for two hours,
until the four holes in the huge planks were scrubbed clean—
not, of course, as the maid at home would have done; we had

no sandpaper, no soap, and no hot water—but when the corporal came to inspect it, he seemed satisfied, finding fault only with the inner edge of the toilets which we had not scrubbed.

"Don't be afraid of the water; there is plenty in the ocean," he said with a grin, and left.

I had never touched such filth in my life, and my good suit, a tailored birthday gift from Aunt Veronica, was splashed and drenched, and so was Hilgers's. He said dryly, "I never knew that a man begins to be a man in the latrine!"

When we came back, a huge kettle of potatoes stood in the middle of our quarters, beside it a smaller one of *Blutwurst* (blood sausage). It was comical to see us in our Sunday best waiting in line to receive three potatoes boiled in their skins, and a piece of *Blutwurst* in a metal bowl. The corporal himself handed out and mashed the *Blutwurst* onto my potatoes, so that it burst and the reddish stuff oozed out on both sides. He grinned as he did this; but when I, trying to be jovial, grinned back, he instantly gave his face an uncanny expression by dropping the lid of his right eye to make it appear very small. Was my smile not in good form?

I withdrew into a corner. Hungry as I was, I could eat only the potatoes. It seemed to me as if the *Blutwurst* had the odor of the latrine. I was astonished when, on my way to the garbage can, I was asked for the *Blutwurst* by a fellow who swallowed it with great gusto before my big eyes. I was thankful when I could climb onto the third tier where my bunk was; I was so tired I couldn't even say my childhood prayer: *Müde bin ich, geh' zur Ruh'* . . . (I am tired, go to rest . . .).

The next morning, at the command "Rise" and the clamor of shoes walking over the squeaky boards, I realized I was a soldier now—the Kaiser's soldier. I jumped down to dress. It was still dark outside. No sooner had I put on my trousers than the corporal asked Hilgers and me to bring the coffee and continue such service for the next eight days. He said, loudly enough for all to hear, "The fellows will appreciate your serving them."

The tub was so heavy that we dragged it more than carried it. There was hardly time enough left for us to eat a piece of bread, let alone have a piece of my aunt's cake, for the corporal now cried, "Make up your beds!" He showed us once more with inimitable skill how to tuck in the corners and make the mattress and blankets look like a long, flat box. Naturally, many beds, including mine, did not find favor and had to be remade several times.

When daylight shot through the high windows of the dance hall, the corporal marched with us to the supply depot where uniforms were issued. Alas, not the gray battle uniform for me. A sergeant and three helpers looked at us for a second, then called out a number, whereupon trousers and coats were flung into our arms from a counter. Only the boots were tried on—not an easy matter; those my size were new and the leather stiff.

Returning to our quarters, we had to change into our uniforms and mail our suits home in the packages we had brought for that purpose. Now where to put my cake? I decided to wrap it in paper and put it on my shelf.

At last I had my uniform. It was not new; the black trousers, though not patched, had a rusty sheen in the back. The red collar of the dark blue coat had a worn fringe and the white linen of the cap was yellowed around the band from sweat, but it was the Kaiser's uniform, and I was proud to wear it, as probably hundreds before me had done. I wondered how many of them had already won the Iron Cross.

In the afternoon, we were given guns and cleaning materials. When, later, I sat down to the evening meal, consisting of a bowl of lentil soup, *Kommiss brot* (black bread), and a piece of cheese, which was to cover the morning ration also, I saw most of the others go back to refill their bowls. I envied them.

Presently our corporal, who had eaten in separate quarters behind the dance hall, passed me, and gave Hilgers his bowl to wash, and then he proceeded to the bulletin board to read. If I could only fathom what was in his mind! He was slender, not quite as tall as I, and perhaps nineteen years old. He had thick black hair and a long, thin nose which made him look more Roman than German. He must have been a volunteer and wounded, for he had a slight limp. In general, he was delicately proportioned and had handsome, spiritual features, such as a pianist or a painter might have, except for the grin that gave him a cynical and uncouth look.

The next morning, I found my bed torn open again and my cake on the floor. Without mentioning me, he thundered, "If you want to baby yourself, do it so no one sees it. A beer bottle would look better on the shelf than chocolate," and as if it were an afterthought, he said with a grin, "And I would not mind if such a bottle should find its way to my bed." Where his bed was I found out that same evening after a two-hour march to town to get us used to our boots. Hilgers and I were ordered—he said it was an honor—to clean out his room.

While I was sweeping under his bed, Hilgers found a stained and sticky handkerchief in the corner. As he dangled it before my eyes with a grin, in came its user. He tore it from Hilgers's fingers and stuck it in his pocket. Hilgers immediately busied himself with dusting off a shelf laden with cookies, chocolate, and beer bottles. The corporal then pushed my head down under the bed with the words, "Crawl under it, or don't you wish to do a good job?"

When I rose, I instinctively brushed the dust off my chest, and he yelled, "Thou swine—to poison me with your dirt—do it outside!"

Hurrying out, I heard him scream, "Keep those midwife fingers of yours away from my shelf! Get out of here!"

While Hilgers and I brushed each other off outside, I ventured to suggest that we give the corporal an opportunity to know us better and invite him the next Sunday evening to a swank place for supper. Hilgers thought I was naïve, and said that I might try to befriend the corporal while he would pray for him. "Let us see which one of us gets the farthest."

In the evening, when the corporal was sitting at the table reading the papers, I had my cake, cookies, and chocolate passed on a piece of paper from man to man. All the others helped themselves, but when the corporal's turn came, without looking up he shoved the paper along to the next man.

The first week as a soldier deflated many of my ideals, but I did not waver; in order to ease the burden of my frustrations, I wrote weekly letters to my sister Gretel, in the form of a diary.

My life with Corporal Nippke crept along on its belly like the serpent to which was said, "Upon thy belly shalt thou go, and dust shalt thou eat all the days of thy life."

One rainy afternoon as we marched home tired and wet, after having practiced how to throw ourselves down for cover on the field at a moment's notice, we were running the last hundred yards to our quarters when the yell "Down!" burst upon our ears—exactly as I was about to jump over a puddle. How I looked when I rose up with my blue uniform and my rifle! I had to use my free time after dinner to clean and dry my clothing in front of the big kettle in the kitchen. Several others met with the same misfortune, but when we stood at roll call, the corporal said to me, "You are the only one that hasn't polished his buttons."

I answered that my coat was still damp, and the corporal yelled at the top of his lungs, *"Maul halten!"* ("Shut your mouth!")

This was the last time that I ventured an answer, and I said later to Hilgers, "I failed; you try!"

He smiled and said, "I pray for him every night; the mills of God grind slowly, but they grind exceedingly small."

I was always glad when my platoon joined the others in exercises, for then the friendly staff-sergeant-lieutenant was in command. The day before, for the first time, I saw, high on horseback, the commander of the battalion, Lieutenant First Class Krug.

Our corporal, when asked by a fellow who had good standing —being from the same home town—whether our commander was an active officer, answered for all to hear, "He is an opera singer in civilian life."

Why did he grin so derisively? He had probably never heard an opera. Besides, so many German officers in active service had been killed or wounded in the first few months of the war that the reserve officers had to be called. Would they all be like our commander? He had such a broad smile and his eyes sparkled when he rode along our lines as if he were thanking us for our silent applause! His gleaming epaulets on his broad shoulders gave him a striking dignity. He must have been an imposing figure on the stage. That he was my commander made me forget the corporal—but the corporal did not forget me!

That evening, the corporal inspected the rifles and, finding some barrels not shiny enough, he made five of us, including Hilgers and me, clean the kitchen, scrub the entrance steps to our quarters, and pick up papers around the inn. He also found fault with my hair—it was too long; I should have it cut short. I didn't answer, and he yelled in my ear, "*Jawohl!*" I replied, "*Jawohl,*" and then he said, "Go outside and yell it ten times so I can hear you."

I did so, and Hilgers said to me, "The length of your hair makes you taller than he is."

I pressed Hilgers's hand. How good it was to have a companion in misery!

On a Monday, not more than a week later, we were marching

in the Salzuflen vicinity. Coming back, Corporal Nippke ordered goosestep four times. Each time, a window would open and a girl look out, as though our boots on the cobblestones paid homage to her.

It was at noon heat and, arriving at our quarters, we did not rush for our soup as usual but tried to get rid of our boots. I had been cautious enough not to wear socks, and had wrapped my feet in white flannel; yet, like some others who had new boots, I could not get them off. Though a fellow offered his services to me, I dared not be helped, since the corporal was around. At last I used a chair, on which Hilgers sat, as a boot-jack, and the corporal promptly yelled, "Look at the milkfaces—they think they are outwitting me!"

Try as I might, I could not remove the boots and, returning from afternoon drill, I had to limp. I had hardly reached our quarters when I was ordered to the corporal's room—which I knew well, having cleaned it for eight days. Every nerve seemed to quiver, and the pallid face had lines drawn from the nose around the chin, as if carved with the edge of a knife.

"You limped."

"Yes, sir."

"You wanted to make fun of me."

"No, sir."

"In Belgium I was wounded on the heel by shrapnel. I have reason to limp."

"My feet are sore."

"Pull off your boots. If that is not true, you will carry the food tubs again, three times a day for four weeks." He ordered two of the strongest boys to pull off my boots. The sight impressed him; pieces of skin were worn off and the heels blistered. He shook the boots and sand fell out. We had climbed sandy slides in the woods that afternoon. "It seems to me you were trying to get to the infirmary."

"No, sir."

"Shut up! You knew very well we would have a twelve-mile march tomorrow with thirty-pound packs—answer me!"

"I did not know, sir."

"Liar! It was announced this morning." I learned later he had spoken of it casually to his favorite group of five men, who would watch his eyes for the slightest indication of a wish and jump to fulfill it.

Tuesday morning, I limped to the infirmary; the twenty-minute walk was very painful, and for an hour I had to stand waiting in a line of naked men. Only one voice was heard. It came from a stout, baldheaded major with the golden staff of Aesculapius on his silvery epaulets. He was sitting in an armchair, the ribbon of the Iron Cross in his second buttonhole. I was awed to be in the presence of a doctor who, though the war was not yet a year old, had won the distinction of bravery in the front line.

My turn came. I held my hands close to my naked thighs and stood at attention, lifting my right foot and wheeling around on my left. I heard him say to his aide, "He cannot walk—we will make him run—three spoons!"

I was pushed, rather than moved, forward to the next room, where a sergeant was awaiting me with a bottle and a spoon in his hand, and, commanding three times, "Open, swallow—open, swallow—open, swallow," he gave me castor oil.

After a shower, I was put into a clean bed in a small barracks all alone. Soon I was in such distress I felt as if my heart, my lungs, and everything else in my body were trying to leave me. I could not help thinking of a nurse who replied, when the doctor asked her if the medicine had made the patient's bowels move, "Yes, once before he died and twice after."

This purge had no effect on my blisters; they kept me in bed for several days. As he who enjoys the rainbow will not curse the rain, I, enjoying every minute of this rest and leisure which

I spent writing letters and even composing poems, did not curse the blisters and Corporal Nippke.

The second morning, I received a roommate, also a one-year man, a volunteer who had already seen battle in Lorraine. He had contracted bronchitis and, after being in several hospitals at the rear, had been sent here to the garrison for further treatment. He said he hoped he had T.B. so that he would never have to return. The winter in the Argonne had been severe, and they had lain in trenches filled with water and ice. Their food was wurst, marmalade, pea soup, and turnip soup, but the officers in the casinos had the choicest steaks and French wine. Crown Prince Wilhelm, commander of our army, was enriching the French population behind the front with German babies. Iron Crosses rained upon the officers, while rarely would a sergeant or an ordinary soldier get one.

"Look at that fat doctor of ours sitting there with his Iron Cross," my roommate cried. "He was at the front—to be correct, six miles behind the front line—for only two months. How did he get it? When the colonel of his regiment wished to attend the wedding of his daughter, who was to marry an adjutant of the Crown Prince, the regiment's doctor gave him sick leave, receiving in return the Iron Cross. And that was not all. He was allowed to exchange the front for this lovely Salzuflen, where no bomb, no mortars would molest him for the rest of the war." The whole night, I visualized in the dark Corporal Nippke's twisting face, with his uncanny eye staring at me from beneath its half-closed lid, like that of a Chinese. He may have been wounded, but only slightly, in the thick of battle. He may have witnessed, too, those injustices at the front. Little wonder that he hated Hilgers and me, who he thought were soon to be elevated to the status of officers privileged at his expense.

My comrade had not yet finished his gloomy report. The next morning, he predicted that we would lose the war, not from without, but because of the different treatments accorded the soldiers and the officers. He contrasted the genius of Joffre, who won the battle of the Marne, with the stupidity of our general. Raising his curly blond head from the pillow, he shouted, "Our commander made us race into France without allowing us to stop for breath; and when suddenly we encountered a wall of enemy soldiers, we were too exhausted to strike and were mowed down before food or reinforcements could reach us." I was so afraid the sergeant might hear his disclosures that I changed the topic. Naturally that which fills the heart pours forth from the mouth.

As men with higher education, we were attracted to each other. He had studied engineering, but would—"as sure as the Elbe flows into the North Sea"—finish his studies in America and stay there for good. Because he was a baron, I asked him what would become of his estates. He replied caustically, "They will go to my oldest brother, but they are loaded with debts—let the Kaiser have my share—if there is still a Kaiser." The same day, he was moved to a separate room. Was it because of his lungs, or his defeatism?

My heart became so heavy that I sent a telegram to a friend, Alfred H., in Essen. He came Sunday, bringing chocolate cake and wine, and sat by me the whole day. I had secretly scorned Alfred, whom the draft boards had rejected on account of flat feet—which, however, had never hindered his roaming through the woods with me. Now I almost envied his civilian status, and I told him about Corporal Nippke. At the end of my story, he said, "God bless my flat feet for a long time to come!"

The next morning, I was discharged, but not without one more spoonful of castor oil for a souvenir, to remind me not to come back. That afternoon, practicing on the rifle range, I had to leave twice, and when the staff-sergeant-lieutenant learned that I had just come from the infirmary, he smiled understandingly and sent me back to my barracks. Hell broke loose that evening because I was in bed when my platoon returned. Nippke told me to get up—he had not been notified that I was sick— and ordered me to serve the food for the next eight days, but when he saw how weak I was he ordered me back to bed, fearing that I would fall and spill the food, and return to the infirmary for more vacation.

A package arrived from Aunt Veronica with homemade cookies and chocolate. She wished me to continue with my "bribes of love." In a postscript saying that Gretel was helping her send packages, she asked me to send the names of one or two poor comrades in the company. If my aunt only knew that we had no time to learn anything of our neighbors to the left or right, except to see whether or not they were breathing! Besides, would not Nippke's lynx eye notice the packages and accuse me of trying to be friends with them so I could talk about him?

Poor Hilgers! During a march with the entire battalion, he changed his rifle from the right side to the left because a wasp had stung his right arm. The corporal, though not in command, had spied this breach of discipline. As a result, Hilgers had to clean the corporal's room another eight days! Accompanying me that evening to the post office, Hilgers made a statement so remarkable that I wrote it down, for it showed Nippke from a different angle.

He said, "If you have any doubt that there is a heaven, think of this hell, the existence of which you cannot deny. Just as angels do, demons also try to possess us, and Nippke is the playground of demons."

No sooner said than proven! Our platoon was practicing on the rifle range, and while we were lying on the firing line, it was Nippke's duty to place our hands and elbows in the correct position. When he came to me, he spent so much time correcting the tension of my finger before he deemed me worthy to pull the trigger that the officer who was supervising yelled at me, "Are you asleep?"

I was so nervous I could no longer hold the barrel steady and had to leave the line. What a grin on the face of Nippke! Tears came to my eyes. That evening, I studied the manual and discovered that after twenty-four hours a soldier was permitted to make a complaint. One more humiliation and I would act.

The next morning, the sun beamed so brightly through the windows that I said to myself, "Never will Nippke's shadow become so big that it can close out the sun from my heart," and I smiled and hummed to myself.

Is an evil spirit intuitive? I had put my belt on and taken the rifle in my hand when Nippke, quick as a cat, spied a wrinkle on my bed which I had made when I climbed up to adjust my pillow and which I had forgotten to smooth out. He yelled, "You know very well that inspection is due today. You want me to be the goat!"

When we were eating our soup that evening, the inspecting officer came. We rushed to stand at attention before our beds. It was the first sergeant, and he asked questions about the different parts of the rifle, the manual, and the organization of an army. Corporal Nippke's face twisted, for some soldiers had confused the name of our colonel with that of our brigadier general; others had forgotten the number of units in a brigade, a division, and an army corps. The sergeant's voice grew louder and Nippke's facial contortions more severe. At last, Nippke pointed at me, but the feared abuse could not be diverted.

The sergeant flung at him, "I can pick out my own men. You better see that the others know the answers."

However, he did put the questions to me, and I explained, from the platoon up, the organization of the army, giving the name of the officer at the head of each unit, beginning with our captain and ending with the general of our army corps.

He asked my name and then barked, "I've seen enough of

Germany's last hope." After a threatening look at us wretched recruits, he pulled out his notebook asking, "How many 'one-year men' are in this platoon?"

Nippke snapped his heels. "Two! Herr Feldwebel."

Hilgers and I stepped forward and were briefed that we should keep ready, since we would soon be called to leave for the four-week officers' training course in Paderborn.

That evening, many thanked me for having saved the honor of the platoon. Some, however, said that if they had been in my boots, they would not have answered—just for meanness.

"If you are Nippkized, Nippkize right back," whispered one. Thus the term "Nippkism" was born.

Near the end of our stay in Salzuflen, Hilgers and I took an afternoon walk through the *Kurgarten,* where we found so many officers that we became tired of saluting. In spite of the concert, we left early to take refuge in a people's restaurant and drink our *Apfelrose* in calm assurance that no lieutenant would pass our table to make us jump up and stand at attention. We had not been sitting there long when a voice called, "Hermanns, Hilgers, come here!" I little thought that even this day of rest would bear out the saying "The Devil knows no holiday."

There, near the dance floor, sat our corporal and three others, each with his girl. Nippke wanted to order beer for us, but we refused, saying it would not go well with the applerose we had just drunk. He then told his friends that we used to have governesses, but he had made men of us, and for that we should thank him and pay for a round of beers. We were embarrassed and wished nothing more than to return to our table, but a drunken man sometimes seems to have a sixth sense, and he bellowed, "Don't think you can leave before I tell my story!"

He went on to tell how he had made us, still in civilian clothes, clean the toilets. All at the table chuckled in amusement except one girl who said that if she had been given that order she would have refused to obey. Nippke swallowed the rest of his beer in a gulp and shouted, "Refuse? I'll show you how much they can refuse. Both bend your knees ten times."

We were stunned. Warning him that a staff sergeant was dancing nearby, one of the other corporals interfered, but Nippke, lowering his right eyelid, said to me, "You have the best brains of any in my platoon. You know the manual, don't you?"

I promptly answered, "Yes, sir," but caught myself and quickly said, "No, sir," and the girls shrieked with laughter— was it at my expense or his? He took some beer from a passing waiter, drank deeply, and said in a hoarse voice, "My father had twenty-five years in the army and left it a staff sergeant. He is now a policeman. I have had two years and soon must salute these———," using the worst word imaginable.

There was embarrassment even at the surrounding tables, for just as he made this remark, the music had paused. His girl friend tried to calm him down while we paid the waiter and left. I said to Hilgers that we owed it to our honor to report the man, even though, in a way, I had pity for him. Our commander, Krug, the former opera singer, would sympathize with us and call him on the carpet.

Hilgers answered, "Though we cannot make the corporal better, let us not make him worse, but rather be glad that we are the outlet for his sadism."

I told him I did not have a martyr complex, but one of a crusader, and would fight until justice was done, not for my own sake but for that of others.

Corporal Nippke tried one last trick before I left his command. It was drizzling on our way back from the drill field. He, at the head of the platoon, suddenly began to march more slowly until he was opposite me, and then resumed speed. I became alert, and soon came the command, twice, "Down!" Both times I managed to avoid the puddle-filled ruts by dropping to the right or left of them.

After dinner I was brushing my suit with unusual care,

hoping to make a favorable impression on Lieutenant Krug, when I received news from my sister Gretel. She had been reading a letter from Queen Louisa of Prussia, written, in her flight from Napoleon, to her father, the Duke of Mecklenburg-Strelitz, in which the Queen consoled herself with Goethe's famous lines: "Who never ate his bread in tears, who never in grief-filled nights sat weeping on his bed, does not know you, heavenly powers." The next day I left for Paderborn.

Fate willed it that at the end of the course we were returned to Salzuflen, and not, as we expected, sent to the front. We were now officially acknowledged fit to become officers and entitled to sleep in private quarters.

Hilgers had chosen a religious home hidden in a huge park

filled with rose gardens, ponds, and nightingales. My two friends Heines and Ingenhaag moved with me to the home of Baker Brünger, who had five daughters about our own age. These daughters vied with each other in mending our socks, doing our laundry, and cleaning our boots and uniforms. Nippke knew, of course, where we were spending our free time—on which he had so lavishly drawn to make us men. He was still our immediate superior in the platoon and kept us aware of it. During fencing and bayonet practice, he had the most skilled men as my opponents, so that it would be plain to any supervising officer that I was not worthy of commendation. At rifle inspection, he singled me out for special criticism, saying that if he had not had his appendix already taken out, he would think I was pressing it. He laughed at his own joke, and everyone followed suit. I had to smile myself, but already his right eye was squinting, so I immediately stopped.

Soon it was passed around that we would be sent to the front; and Ingenhaag, Heines, and I resolved to give a goodbye party the next Sunday at Brünger's, where the five girls would serve apple, cherry, and prune pies baked especially for us by their father. Each of us could invite two friends, so I asked Hilgers and Corporal Nippke.

After meticulous grooming, I went to him on a Saturday noon, and I stood, clicking my heels at attention, in the doorway of his room. He was lying on his bed without a coat, suspenders down, and shirt open, smoking his pipe. When he saw me, he pulled the pipe out of his mouth quick as a flash.

He had a frightened look on his face as he asked, "What do you want?"

I answered, "Corporal, sir, we who are living at Baker Brünger's are giving a small party. The good baker is furnishing the pies, the coffee, the cakes, the beer, and the smokes, and I should like to invite you."

The look as if he feared I had come to stab him gave way to a smile—but only for a second; then, setting his right eye for action, he said, "Thank you, but I will not come," and I had already turned to leave when he asked, "Did you really think I would come?"

He stuttered more than he spoke. When I turned around and said, "Yes, sir, Corporal," both his eyes almost closed, as if he did not wish to see me.

"I will not come," he repeated.

I clicked my heels and left.

For one more week, I was under his immediate command, but whenever he spoke to me it was in a quiet way.

Once, however, his sarcasm did flare up. When we were packing our knapsacks for the front, by chance, he saw a picture of me in uniform with my sisters Gretel and Hilda. He grinned, which invited the others packing nearby to grin also. "One night with those two would have made me think better of their brother," he said. "Of course, he isn't worth the splinter I got in my leg, and I would be ashamed if he fell for Kaiser and Reich. My family has had generations of master sergeants, and they would turn in the grave had I not come back with a wound from Belgium. 'Why didn't you come home with an Iron Cross, too?' were my father's first words when he visited me in the hospital. We still have my grandfather's Iron Cross hanging under glass in the living room. Hermanns, that sugar face, will be welcomed back with the words 'How good that nothing happened to you.'" He waited for laughter and, after receiving such a reaction, returned to me: "Am I not right, Hermanns?"

In the presence of some twenty smirking soldiers, I said, "*Jawohl.*"

"When can I meet your sisters? Do something for the Fatherland!"

This scene I related at the last kaffee klatsch given by the

Brünger's. Hilgers said, "Willie, if I were you, I would give him something better than your sisters. Write him a 'goodbye' letter and put in the thoughts we have discussed so often."

This letter I put in his room when I left for the front:

Dear Corporal Nippke:

Our relationship, so you expressed last week in the presence of half the platoon, would have been better had you met my two sisters, Gretel and Hilda, instead of me. I well understand your feeling, seeing me in a photo in a tailor-made uniform which one-year soldiers have the right to wear. However, I did not write those regulations which give privileges to one group and not to another. . . . I hope that if you should deny me a tombstone with the inscription "Fallen for Kaiser and Reich," you would not deny me the compliment that I was a good pupil, and what you taught me has made indelible impressions upon my mind, so much so that I will be able to comfort others who may meet another "Corporal Nippke."

III. THE LORD IS NOT LOOKING

We one-year men had been especially informed of the reasons for the invasion of France. In the officers' training school at Paderborn, we had attended lectures by Captain Weinert: "France is full of venereal diseases, and has been sterile since the war of 1870. We of German stock increase by 700,000 births a year. Thus France has forfeited the right to have so much territory in a crowded Europe. With a population exceeding France's by twenty million, we merely obey nature's decree, the survival of the fittest, by wresting from France the living space we need." This message came from the mouth of an authority who, before addressing us every morning from his high pulpit, pulled off each finger of his glove with his teeth because his left hand had been shattered by a bullet. When, once, his glove slid from the desk, the man nearest him eagerly dashed up the five steps to pick it up. (Indeed, it should have been venerated, for was not its wearer a hero?) How he harangued us from the pulpit! Whether he spoke about the famous German strategist Clausewitz or on Germany's war aims, every sentence was short and clipped like a military command, and his arms moved up and down like hammer strokes. His wiry body, his pale boyish face, his black piercing eyes were for me the epitome of the German officer.

How he despised cowardice! In 1914, during the invasion of Belgium, he told us in another lecture, "I discovered a man who hesitated to attack with drawn bayonet, so that evening I had him placed at an advanced post on the top of the hill, knowing well what would happen. Sure enough, the next morning he was found with bullets through his body. An offensive cannot brook cowardice." When saying this, he gently touched the black and white ribbon of his Iron Cross with his crippled fingers.

This Hauptmann Weinert—what an example to emulate! At the training school's farewell banquet, all aspirant officers vowed in a toast never to forsake what he had taught us.

No sooner had five of my companions and I rejoined the company than the call came to advance to the Western Front. It was the end of July and very hot. As an *Ersatzbattalion,* we were to replace the casualties in the 67th Regiment. At every village and town we passed, we hung out the train windows to wave and yell as though we were going to a *Kirmes*. From every compartment roared the song "Victoriously we will crush France and die as brave heroes." When we reached a point just past the border of Luxembourg, however, we had to leave the train—our train was needed on the other front. We had to walk the remaining distance to the lines, a march of several days. Passing through a charming French town near a castle with terraced rose gardens whose perfume filled the streets, we were suddenly ordered to change our gait to a goose-step. A cluster of generals was waiting ahead to receive this honor. My comrade Hilgers nudged me. "There is Field Marshal Count von Haeseler."

I saw a parchment face that looked as if it belonged to a shriveled-up woman, except for the eyes—the young and alert eyes, riveted on the rows of passing soldiers. His uniform, that of the uhlans, was magnificent. The huge epaulets glittered with gold. I felt proud to meet history in a man who had already seen three victorious wars.

A younger man stood beside him. Someone said it was General von Mudra. But it was the medals which held my thoughts. When would I win mine? One sparkling medal, fastened at an officer's throat, caught my eye. It was probably the Order *Pour le Mérite,* in gold oak leaves and crossed swords, strewn with diamonds. Only the Kaiser himself, I thought, could award such a high medal.

We had heard in our officers' course that the counsel and support of the veteran Field Marshal and the finest strategists of the military General Staff had been made available to the young Crown Prince. This befitted the dynastic glory of the yet inexperienced man with the title of Imperial and Royal Highness. Now I was goosestepping before these guarantors of German victory.

As I marched on, I recalled having seen the Kaiser and the Crown Prince several times on horseback, followed by a large retinue of officers. But always, when the Kaiser drew nigh, I had eyes only for him. What else was there for a young boy to behold, especially since he was named after this same Kaiser? And did not every man in the ancient fortress at Koblenz, from commanding general to postman, wear his stiff mustache upturned in the Kaiser's style?

Recollecting my childhood, I remembered that the Crown Prince was not a popular figure in the western part of Germany. Twice he had struck a wrong note. The first incident occurred in 1913 when he banned Gerhart Hauptmann's play, written for the centennial of the battle of Leipzig, because the playwright alluded to the brotherhood of all men. I agreed with my sister Gretel and my Aunt Veronica that he had no right to limit a poet's expression. Later, he caused a second upset in our household with his part in the notorious Zabern Affair. He had sided with a young lieutenant who had insulted the Alsatians, former French citizens. Again I agreed with my family, for they called him a Prussian saber rattler who needed to learn something from the freedom-loving people settled in western Germany around the Rhine Valley.

Now, however, I said to myself, Let the loyalty that I swore to the Kaiser and the Reich as a newly enlisted soldier not be tarnished by a critical attitude toward a man who would be largely responsible for this war's outcome. Recently, a medal had been struck in gold with an effigy of the Crown Prince as a German Siegfried, wearing a bearskin over his naked body. His muscular arm was stretched high over his head, swinging a club. A bear, a serpent, and a lion lay cringing under his mighty feet—a symbol of future victories over Russia, France, and England. Also the 5-pfenning postcards carried his image in his uniform of the Death's-Head Hussars, with skull and crossbones on his shako. Now, assigned to the Fifth Army, the Crown Prince was my commander. My fate lay in his hands. He had suddenly become a magic figure. My uniform was his, and his honor mine.

When we stopped to rest that night in an old French army barracks, we all were given cigarettes—a gift from the Crown Prince.

The next day, we soldiers were footsore from marching, and I was tempted to catch a ride on the baggage wagon as some others did. But experience held me back. I still recalled vividly the time in Salzuflen when I went to the infirmary for treatment of sore feet and was given three spoonfuls of castor oil, "to learn how to run." How could I be sure that this would not happen again? Others were hobbling, too, so I hobbled on.

As we were marching the following day, the charming villages with their greenery and gardens, occasional mansions, and villas gave way to roofless buildings, mutilated churches, and devastated landscapes. Why should it bother us after all our training for war? We must get accustomed to it. We marched through the ruins singing all the louder, *"Deutschland über Alles."*

When we reached the village of Passy-Haut, a peasant woman holding two children gazed at us with a mute hatred that fastened itself in my mind. Somewhere in that vicinity, we were billeted in a barn. Roaming with a few comrades, I found three skeletal corpses near a cemetery wall. Two of the dead men wore blue peasant smocks; the third wore the cassock of a priest. As we talked about this later in the barn, Hilgers and I were horrified to hear a soldier say, "Only three hostages? Last year in Dinant, a sniper shot one of our officers. We sealed up the street, set fire to the houses, and whoever ran out was shot." I thought of the woman with the two children, and of the hatred in her face.

On the next day's march, into the Argonne Forest, the singing slowed down. The war was not the "brisk and jolly war" that the Crown Prince had proclaimed in 1914. When we passed the village of Apremont, the Argonne Forest lay before us, but we saw none of the saturated verdure of the lush summer. We heard no woodpeckers, nor did we see wild pigs or deer running through thickets. We saw none of the animals that had made the forest famous as a royal hunting ground. The mighty trees, centuries old, stood beheaded. Much of the underbrush was charred; the valleys, hills, and ridges were scarred by trenches.

After my first night in this place, I discovered that desolation was not limited to nature. Returning from the latrine, I noticed that my new blanket had disappeared, and with it the new underwear from my knapsack. Instead, an old blanket, full of lice, was thrown on my cot. I went to Master Sergeant Hoehne in his office. With a cynical smile, he said, "Well, that's a good toughening-up for you who want to become officers."

The same afternoon, I found that my rifle had vanished just

as the whistle was blown for roll call and weapon inspection. In front of the entire company, Sergeant Hoehne with his wry smile told me, "At midnight we have to go to the front. You have till then to procure another rifle." As I sat in the barracks, I remarked that the sergeant could have found my rifle during roll call by checking its serial number. A seasoned soldier said, "Why should he? You came with a new rifle. We have old rusty ones. Someone stole yours. Now you have to go and steal someone else's." I was horrified. Had I come here to be robbed by my comrades and then stand there with no one to help in my plight? How could I steal a rifle without getting caught? I looked around—nothing but ominous slopes with dense underbrush and tree stumps. I made my way through the woods for an hour until I came to the quarters of a company whose men were building trenches. I sneaked inside a tent, picked up a rifle, and hurried back. In a deep ravine, not far from my company's quarters, I tripped over a spiked helmet and noticed it marked a grave. I sat down beside it and wondered what kind of thoughts had occupied the man's mind before he took his last breath. The rifle weighed heavier and heavier.

A picture of a theft from my childhood came to me. I was then a boy of five. I was sent with my sister Gretel to fetch Anna, the maid, who was walking my baby sister Hilda in the Rhine Garden in Koblenz. It looked as if it might rain, so my mother pressed little umbrellas into our hands. Since the clouds were breaking up, and I wanted my hands to be free, I gave the umbrellas to a poor boy sitting in front of the statue of General von Goeben, which passed on our way to the Rhine. "Keep these umbrellas for us until we come back," I told him. "Here are ten pfennigs for you."

Amusing ourselves by skipping stones on the Rhine, we arrived late at the place where Anna usually sat with the baby, near the statue of the Empress Augusta. Anna and Hilda had already gone. And so had the boy with our two umbrellas. Gretel and I then hurried to the poor sections of town, asking everyone if they had seen a boy with bare feet, patched trousers, and two umbrellas. We went to the *Deutsches Eck*, where the Moselle flows into the Rhine, and asked the fishermen. Then, to be alone, we climbed to the topmost step of the colossal monument to Wilhelm I. The world had suddenly become a terrible place. Gretel was weeping and wanted to go home.

When we arrived, I found my mother with little Hilda crying on her arm. Fearing an accident had befallen us, she had sent the maid, the cook, and three or four others to search for Gretel and me. My mother embraced me, wetting my cheeks with her tears. But I tore myself loose and shouted, "Mother, I gave the umbrellas to a boy to hold for us, and he kept them! I didn't know he was so bad." In my young life, this was my first disappointment with human nature—to discover that people could be deceitful.

And now I myself was forced to act the same way as that little barefooted thief. But here, sitting by this soldier's grave, I could contemplate a difference: the boy was entirely unaware of the fear and grief he caused by stealing our umbrellas, and I was only too aware of the consequences of taking someone else's rifle. In my mind's eye, I could foresee a series of poor soldiers like me, each stealing from the next. And the worst of it was that my own theft could have been prevented. There were plenty of extra weapons collected from the dead and wounded; the sergeant could have issued me a rifle with just a word.

I almost envied this dead soldier whose grave I seemed to guard, for all his problems of conscience were over. And, like that day when I was five years old, sitting on the steps of the monument, now, too, I did not want to go back to face people again.

I held the helmet for a long time. Finally, I said to the dead soldier, "Did they also tell you, 'When you join the army you become a man'?"

Walking slowly from his grave to my barracks, I wondered how much bitterness and resentment a soldier could endure before he must revolt.

That evening, lying on my back, I was told by Unteroffizier Schell, who had three years' service—two in peace and one in war—that I shouldn't make such a fuss about stealing a rifle. "Besides," he said, "the *Spiess* [Master Sergeant Hoehne] didn't say you should *steal* a rifle, but *procure* one. A soldier doesn't steal. What would you do if you had to shoot a hostage? I have done so many a time in Belgium, and if I were ordered to shoot you because you refused to go forward, I would do so."

Some other seasoned soldiers chimed in that the Prussian State had made us Germans what we are today—powerful and feared. I should not forget that God has always been on the side of the State. One, a high school teacher, boasted that he told his pupils in history hour that "God had the Russian Empress Elizabeth, that whore, die at the moment Frederick the Great was losing the Seven Years' War. Then Catherine came to the throne and made peace with Frederick. She never forgot that she was a German princess."

This was too much for me, and I said that Frederick the Great had had his experience with the power of conscience, though not his own. "He ordered one of his officers to sack the castle of Count Brühl in Saxony out of pure revenge. And you can still read on the tombstone of this officer, von der Marwitz, near Berlin, that he preferred to follow his honor rather than the order of the King."

Schell blew out the candle. "That officer should have been shot. Our Kaiser could not fight a war if everyone would first consult his own conscience. Hermanns, you ought to know by now that whatever a soldier is ordered to do, he does. The Lord is not looking."

The teacher added, "Victory is ours. It has already been well fixed in the Reichstag what the French, Belgians, and Russians have to pay after the war is over. My father belongs to the national party and has sent me clippings about the sessions which decided these indemnities."

I was stunned. "And you think the Lord says yes to that, too?"

"Shut up, Hermanns. It is better to be eaten by lice than by one's own conscience. Steal or procure, extort or demand—who cares? We are winning the war."

I now had a suspicion who was probably wearing the new underwear which I had brought from home. I sank into my own thoughts while the teacher began to lecture in the dark about Frederick the Great's genius. Suddenly I felt a poking at my head. He had reached down from the upper tier and bellowed in my face. "Mark the words of our great King: 'First I get what I can and then I have my lawyers prove that I am right.'" This led me to think that these people here were so entrenched in the belief of the State that it was virtually impossible for them to confront their own consciences. And moreover, if man's conscience can be so systematically blunted in the army, couldn't a rifle, which a man is ordered to steal, someday direct a bullet not at the enemy but at one's hated superior? Master Sergeant Hoehne may well breed hate in someone more revengeful than I.

Something else startled me. This Unteroffizier Schell, with his pale blue eyes, almost sickly complexion, and subdued voice, boasted of having killed hostages and would kill me, too, if they ordered, just like that!

I poured forth my heart in a letter to my sister Gretel that evening. I wrote, "I have come here to be loyal to the Kaiser and Reich, but something happened to me that makes me feel that I have been spiritually mutilated, like the miserable, broken, bare trees here in the forest."

My sister answered with a poem from my late mother's verse book, and my Aunt Veronica tried to comfort me in her own way: "Every evening when I look out the window to the east toward Russia, I say, 'There is Hans [my brother] and Otto, Jacob, and Siegfried [my cousins].' I turn to the west and say, 'There is Willie, my boy, in the Argonne, Hugo and Fritz in the Champagne, and I pray for them all. Don't worry, Willie. I feel God will send you back to me.'" Would He? I wondered when I read her letter. She had also prayed for her nephew George, and he had fallen on the first day of the invasion of Belgium. To me, prayers were as mysterious as the Argonne Forest, for there seemed to be no way out. Who could know whether my helmet would not soon lie in a bare patch in the underbrush?

With the flying shells, the dynamiting of the trenches, the incessant rains, snow, and hail, and the ankle-deep mud everywhere, it was difficult to tell which caused more deaths, the ravages of nature, with disease and exhaustion in their wake, or destruction by man. At Christmas, General von Mudra told us, "Your Christmas bells are the thundering guns. Your Christmas trees are the mutilated firs."

We died slowly, unheroically. White crosses sprouted up beside stumps of trees. I remembered the Kaiser's proclamation of the previous June: "The triumph of the greater Germany, which someday must dominate all Europe, is the single end for which we are fighting." And for the first time I thought about the words "greater Germany." Was its triumph to be a nation of cemeteries?

In the summer of 1915, our 34th Division managed to conquer a trench from the enemy, an advance of a hundred yards, but even this small victory, so rare in the Argonne Forest, caused more grief than joy. Our batteries, not yet informed that the trench was ours, fired on our position, killing and wounding twenty-eight. Such was the confusion in our forward trenches that we no longer knew if we were throwing grenades at the French or at our neighboring company.

Even more disheartening was the news from behind the lines. We learned that ammunition sent for our batteries, already piled in protective gorges in the forest, was reloaded and taken to other fronts. We saw, too, that because of heavy losses among our infantry officers in the Argonne, cavalry officers, after short training, filled the gap. Then I learned another stunning fact. We were attacking with poison gas in defiance of the Geneva agreements. We must have become desperate indeed.

General von Mudra had said, "What is ours we keep; where we advance with our bayonets we tear the enemy to pieces." These words had no more resonance in us. And the famous German song beginning, "Argonne Forest, at midnight a pioneer stands on lonely watch . . ." no longer was sung in our barracks. Gone was the romantic world of nightingales and soft breezes. This was the real world of dirt and desolation.

One day my detachment was ordered to build a communication trench to the front. It was raining heavily as we began work. Suddenly we must have struck a well, for water gushed into the diggings with such force that we had to jump out of the trench into plain sight of the French to avoid drowning. That instant a black-winged monster came flying toward us— an air torpedo, which we called *Schusterschemel*. We all jumped back. The bomb tore a crater close by, and uprooted a tree stump which landed on the head of our Corporal Weihe. His body was thrown into the ditch and his head was hammered into the mud. We pulled him out, but before we could clear the mud from his throat he suffocated.

As we dug closer to the forward positions, we were forced to work at night for safety. Without speaking, under the blackness of skies piled with low-hanging, rain-soaked clouds, we cut through mud, loam, and roots with picks and shovels. One night we reached a crater so immense that a two-story house could have been placed in it. There we saw something that petrified us. At the bottom stood the upright figure of a man wearing red trousers. We called with muffled voices, "Comrade, comrade."

Our front man wanted to throw a hand grenade, but we held him back. By the light of a flare floating overhead just then, we noticed that neither the red trousers nor the bayonet moved. After we had carefully walked down into the crater, we stood transfixed, just as did this phantom—or had it become two? For on the end of his bayonet a body was impaled—legs, torso, and head standing upright, held erect partly by the knee-deep mud and partly by two bayonets. This man, too, was holding a rifle with fixed bayonet piercing his killer. Since the second phantom wore gray, we had not discovered him until we were only yards from the red-trousered corpse. The German must have jumped into the crater to pierce the Frenchman, but overlooked the waiting bayonet. The odor was so strong and nauseating that we pressed our handkerchiefs against our faces and climbed out of the crater.

After a while, Corporal Adamiack climbed back with three men, chosen by lot, to separate the skewered bodies. When they pulled them apart, the bayonets slid from their impaled chests and dropped in the mud, along with the bodies. Then we all went down to shovel them underground. As we worked, we noticed a little chain with a Madonna beneath the Frenchman's shirt. But no one dared touch it for fear that part of his flesh would tear off with it.

Nonetheless Adamiack had us take all the belongings from the dead men's pockets. The odor of these objects was so powerful we had to disinfect them with urine before rinsing them with water.

THE LORD IS NOT LOOKING

I had become used to the infernal rumblings of cannons as I slept in the daytime, but the specter of the Frenchman's Madonna robbed me of sleep. The Frenchman had put his faith in her. And yet, while defending his soil, he was killed, but not without managing to lance the heart of his attacker while he was dying. Two men who had never seen each other had been taught that they were enemies. Perhaps the German was Catholic, too. Did they both pray to God for victory in battle?

I remembered words of the Kaiser framed in gold in my classroom in the Empress Augusta Gymnasium in Koblenz: "We shall conquer everywhere, even though we be surrounded by enemies on all sides; for there lives a powerful ally, the good old God in heaven, who . . . has always been on our side."

This same God filled the lips of the chaplains whenever we heard their sermons behind the front, and I wondered if at the same time the French weren't having a similar sermon, claiming God as *their* "powerful ally."

Even the Crown Prince occasionally took part in divine services, in which he or the minister spoke of the "unfading laurels" with which everyone in the Argonne Forest had covered himself. In the field service on July 27, he said: "We shall cover the back of our comrades on the Eastern Front with God's help. And do it until it is possible to get the French at bay. I know I can rely on you, and I thank you for this in the name of His Majesty, the supreme war lord, hooray, hooray, hooray." This kind of God, I thought, is worthy to be worshiped by sheep. And is the German soldier not made a blind sheep? When we first donned the uniform in Salzuflen, we were told by the master sergeant, who boasted that he could trace his lineage of master sergeant back to Frederick the Great, "And one thing, remember: a soldier has a duty to obey but he is not allowed to think."

The text of the Crown Prince's speech was mimeographed

and attached to the door of the canteen. Some hand, unkind to the German cause, had affixed a leaflet which had been dropped by the French planes over the German front. "Proclamation to the Poles," it announced. "There is no love lost between you Poles in Prussian military service and your Prussian overlords. Come over to our side. We French soldiers will receive you with all the honors which we had bestowed on a free Poland through the centuries, and which shall be free again, for this war shall be won by us, the Allies. Prussia has to give back to Poland the provinces she has stolen from her, which now form lands of East Prussia, Posnany, and Silesia."

When our master sergeant Hoehne discovered this poster, knowing the culprit could not be found, he ordered the whole company to do distasteful chores for a full day. We should have been resting to be ready for the front.

Ironically, all the Poles from East Prussia, in whose houses Polish was spoken, had been sent to the Western Front to stall desertions to the Russians, whose language they understood. And now they were invited by the French to defect to France. The name "Polack," with which the Germans often stigmatized them, and the name "Wackes," tagged on the soldiers from the Alsace-Lorraine, did not enhance the feelings of loyalty of these minorities conquered in former wars for the Kaiser and Reich.

Theodor Hilgers, our seminarian, said to me that evening as we returned from doing our chores, "This disloyalty of the Poles is the fruit of Frederick the Great's invasion of their Silesia. 'One takes when one can, and one is wrong only when obliged to give back.' Now we are to suffer for the *Weltanschauung* of this atheistic cynic on the throne of Prussia."

But deserters were not limited only to members of minorities. The torrents of rain and snow, the terrible hunger to which our soldiers were subjected in the trenches in the winter of 1915, the knowledge that a rations system had been imposed at home, the stories of starving children—all this undermined the traditional faith in Kaiser and Reich. Thus, two "good Prussians" and a sergeant of Saxony, who were among those engineers ordered to build a tunnel into no man's land and fill it with dynamite, never came back, defecting on the very day we expected the French trench to blow up. I remember Lieutenant Langenkamp, with several battalion officers, watching with binoculars for French bodies to explode into the air. But it was not to happen.

Undoubtedly the safest place for a soldier to be was the hospital. Many were frantic to get there at any cost short of death. It was not uncommon to see a soldier stretch his hand out over the trench during the night in the hope of catching a bullet. I had tried it myself once in a moment of depression.

A friend from Cologne one night took off his boots and stood in ice water to freeze his feet. A few weeks later, I was pleasantly surprised to find myself among those who had contracted furuncles on the legs from standing in water in the trenches. We were sent to a hospital in the rear at Nouillonpont.

There I was appalled at the number of soldiers who were suspected by the doctor of a *Heimatschuss*, a self-inflicted shot to get away from the front. Also, I saw two young German soldiers handcuffed and led by field police to a war tribunal, which, as the war progressed, seemed to grow increasingly punitive.

In Nouillonpont, I was attracted by a village church with its old statues and paintings. A lonely priest would say Mass every morning, sometimes to two or three old women with headcloths covering much of their faces, but most of the time to no one at all. Once I tried to give the women pieces of bread which I had saved from my ration, but they fled away from me. I made the acquaintance of the priest, however, by showing an interest in the twenty beehouses, each painted a different color, which he had behind his parish house. One day I saw him with his bees, wearing a sort of net helmet covering his face, neck, and shoulders, moving through the garden in his long black gown like a Jules Verne creature. He was trying to catch a swarming queen. When I approached, he warned me. From then on, the ice was broken and I visited him several times in his study. About fifty, agile, small, with his pince-nez bouncing on his nose, he could have been a twin brother of our Major Warnberg, and I told him so. That was the closest we ever came to talking about the war. Any attempt of mine to speak of politics, even of the French victory on the Marne, was met with icy silence. Did he think I was a stool pigeon? The only conversation he liked was about his books: Pascal, Hugo, and St. Augustine.

After four weeks in Nouillonpont, I returned to the Argonne. The low morale of the soldiers must have become known to higher circles, for whenever we would go to the rear for eight days' rest in our rotation from the front line, we found not only delousing plants and shower facilities but also cinemas in abandoned houses that still had roofs. Also, military bands played at noon in the marketplaces.

However, in that village of Saint-Juvin where the band played in front of the officers' mess hall, there were drawbacks. Once we saw officers coming out of the hall, still holding wineglasses in their hands. Through the open door we saw others dancing with one another. A sergeant standing by me spat and said, "I wouldn't be surprised if one of these days this mess hall goes up in flames."

Even the luster of heroic names like Lüttwitz, Brauchitsch, and Hammerstein-Equord among the officers did not improve the stalemate of the "Mudra Corps" in the Argonne. Of course, there were many heroic deeds by officers and men: one officer jumped into an enemy trench with an experimental flame thrower and burned himself to death. Captain von Kloesterlein, with chosen men, sneaked before dawn behind the enemy lines near La Harazée and captured a French platoon. There was the story of the volunteer soldier Surth, who, with his legs blown away by a hand grenade, said, "Let me lie here, comrade—I have to die. Take the machine gun forward and fire upon the French." And there was my own major, Warnberg, with his ludicrous pince-nez bobbing on his nose when he rode horseback, whose indomitable courage made him lead an attack against superior numbers, from which he returned wounded with only a few survivors. And above all was the story of the angry young lieutenant, blood-soaked, with torn coat and only a small piece of his rifle left, who came out of the forest and reported to General von Mudra watching the attack from an observation post of the 135th Regiment, "This advance is impossible! All my men are dead. You have ordered a superhuman task for us." The general, after carefully weighing this information, ordered them to fall back.

When I mentioned this story in the barracks, saying I would like to write a letter to the young lieutenant, congratulating him for his courage, my friend Hilgers said, "Willie! That lieutenant risked court-martial for insubordination in criticizing the army command within earshot of other soldiers."

"If I were the officer presiding at the military tribunal, I would congratulate General von Mudra," I said. I admired General von Mudra from that day on, for he had listened to the pleas of a young lieutenant and had saved lives.

My year's experience in the Argonne was not without comic incidents. One evening, when we had been allotted a piece of bread and one herring to be divided among eight hungry soldiers, I suggested that, instead of dividing the herring into eight little pieces, we should hang the fish by a string and each of us jump for it with open mouth—the prize going to whoever snapped it up. When Lieutenant Langenkamp passed through the trenches and saw the jumping at the entrance of my foxhole, he called me a troublemaking intellectual who would awaken Communist instincts in his fellow soldiers. Apparently, he did not appreciate the sense of humor by which a Rhinelander can mitigate the more tragic aspects of life.

The lieutenant and I were both about twenty years old, of the same height and stature, and had had higher education as well as officers' training, but in the present situation we were worlds apart. There he stood before me in his silky-textured transparent raincoat, showing his tailored uniform with handsome epaulets on the shoulders and gleaming boots that looked as if they had just been shined by his orderly. I wore an old uniform covered with mud and loam, and stood in ragged colorless boots that were stiff with mud. He stood puffing a cigarette in his gloved hand, while I stood at attention, answering, *"Jawohl, Herr Leutnant! Nein, Herr Leutnant!"*

He left me baffled. I barely knew what Communism meant. If my willingness to share what I had with others—a religious principle instilled by Aunt Veronica—made me a Communist, then perhaps the lieutenant had dubbed me correctly. Could it be that Lieutenant Langenkamp sensed our resentment when we fetched our meager rations while observing what the officers' orderlies carried from the quartermaster's stores: steaks, French wines and cheeses, and fresh vegetables, even in winter?

And yet the lieutenant had proved on another occasion that he had no personal feelings against me. He had caught me sleeping at my post when he made an inspection tour of the front line at two o'clock in the morning. At that time, we had barely slept for thirty-six hours because the pouring rain had forced us to bail the trenches constantly to keep from drowning in them or from having the sodden walls of our shelter cave in on us. We were placed about five yards apart in the trenches— each in front of a steel shield with a hole for the gun barrel, and packed in by sandbags. We arranged among ourselves that one

of us would doze in a standing position, while his neighbor would watch for our two adversaries, the French from no man's land and the lieutenant from the rear. We did not have to worry about the noncommissioned officers, for they were sleeping, too, and had to be awakened when danger approached. They needed our benevolence as much as we needed theirs. Langenkamp's gloved hand shook me awake, and he hissed at me from between his teeth: "I could have taken away your rifle and let you sleep on. The French would come, and that would be it for you. I could also court-martial you, but I will not." Then he left. And suddenly I felt differently about him.

We were mummies wrapped in loam, our eyelids so heavy from want of sleep that our glazed eyes barely peered through the lashes. No spark of morale was left. The two armies were like fighting stags with their horns interlocked, doomed to stick together until death.

I felt sorry for the Crown Prince, whose army seemed ill-fated. During the onslaught to Paris, heavy losses befell his army at Longwy. He was checked, although the German newspapers made it appear as a victory. Later, Fort de Troyon barred his way. The losses forced him to break up the attack. Now in the Argonne Forest the situation grew so serious, as our men returning from furlough learned from the "pigs in the rear," that the Chief of the General Staff, General von Falkenhayn, became worried about the losses. In fact, he had gone in person to the headquarters of the Crown Prince that August to complain about the ineffectiveness of the Argonne Corps.

We had fought so hard for many months, and had nothing to show for it but a hill here and a trench there. True, the Crown Prince's army had never been routed, but the mud on our boots seemed to get heavier and heavier, and the words spoken by Field Marshal von Haeseler to wounded soldiers, "You come from the Argonne Forest and I'm afraid you will have to remain there until the war is finished," did not improve our morale. Or, as brave Lieutenant Birkenfeld once said: "I long for the war of movement, where man can face man. This trench warfare is an insult to God, King, and Fatherland." He was wounded that very night. Had God resented the boasted partnership with the Kaiser?

It was with great relief that we learned in the summer of 1916 that our regiment had been ordered to leave the Argonne. This good news was followed up by Master Sergeant Hoehne's summoning the one-year soldiers. He announced that we had a twenty-day leave. Hoehne, pressing furlough money into our hands, remarked matter-of-factly, "You may wish to come back sooner than the twenty days; the food is better here than you can get at home, and where we will go from here it will be better still." He dismissed us with the cynical smile which Hilgers thought he had copied from the Sphinx. Or was it the smile of the Mona Lisa, who, as the story goes, knew a frightful secret?

We unraveled this much: when we returned from furlough, we would become group leaders or even platoon leaders with corresponding promotions, and take the place of officers in the raging battle before Verdun, since the regular officer corps had had so many losses during the first two years of war. The prospect of such carnage did not perplex the military mind, however. The more suicidal the mission, the more valor and glory. As the master sergeant had pointed out, "I only have the misfortune to face you; you will have the privilege to face the enemy. The Iron Cross could be yours." The seven of us had one thought at the time: none of us would go on furlough with the Iron Cross. How inflated our expectations had been when we volunteered at the beginning of the war! What would my girl friend Toni think when she saw me undecorated?

In spite of the furlough, we were gloomy. The bravest of us, Heines, ventured, "I would rather have been sent home for good with a bullet wound in my arm or leg. When we return in a few weeks, we'll be thrown into the battle of Verdun." This battle had been raging since February, and for weeks at a time the Argonne Forest would shake as if a continuous earthquake centered nearby. The Crown Prince, commander of our army, had announced that the Kaiser would dictate the peace terms to France on the cathedral square at Verdun. So far, no victory, no peace. Was it up to our "Mudra Corps" to storm the French fortress? No one knew the truth, but what was in store for us was as thick in our minds as the rumbling in the air.

When I said goodbye to Soldier First Class Brandt, he pressed into my hands a diamond ring he had found in the rubble of a shelled house for his mother to buy food with. Then he read a letter he wanted me to take to her. "Dear Mother: They say we will be sent to Verdun. You have lost two sons in Russia. Whatever happens to me, remember you have given your boys for the Fatherland. I had a terrible dream, I felt as if I had been hit by a bullet and was lying in a shell hole. I could see the blood soaking my uniform and there was no one to help. I pulled out my rosary and your picture, and then I woke up. Mother, pray for me. And should it happen, don't try to find out where it happened or how it happened; just take flowers to my father's grave and know that René, Paul, and I are there."

When midnight neared, I sneaked into the company storeroom behind the kitchen shed and left my knapsack there. I took with me only a pad of writing paper and my diary.

Twenty days later I returned, my diary filled with the account of my trip home. The furlough had been a dream—a bad dream, to be sure—and would have been forgotten as such had it not

THE LORD IS NOT LOOKING

been for Master Sergeant Hoehne and probably Lieutenant Langenkamp. They saw to it that the stories I told would not only cancel my promotion but also transfer me from that company to another one which was deathbound as surely as night follows day—the heavy machine-gun company.

The first night I was back, we were all securely within our bunker, deep in the hidden ravines of the Argonne Valley. A few miles behind the front, artillery fire zoomed over in wide arcs and exploded in the midst of the forest. My comrades pestered me to tell them about my experiences with women.

I immediately read them my notes, happy to please. I did not do so in innocence, because the furlough had made me darkly aware that all was not right in the homeland. I could not let this opportunity pass.

I first told them how at Sedan the train, filled with men on furlough, had to wait for connections for three hours and that a young officer who was also from the Rhineland had treated me as his equal and invited me to the *Puff*.

Two armed soldiers stood at the door, along with a field gendarme. The ominous minion of the law was reminding the customers of this establishment that the military court was close at hand. My companion must have been familiar with the place. Without a word, he walked to the table on his left, received a number, as did I, and then stepped to another table where two sergeants sat, adorned with the Aesculapian symbol and a Red Cross armband. My companion pulled out his penis. One of them pressed it, and the other did the same with mine. A young medic took him immediately down the corridor, since his number had no significance for someone of his rank. I never saw him again. I had to wait in line, but not for long. I realized while walking into door thirteen that the *Puff* had been installed in a barracks divided into cubicles. When I entered the cubicle, I saw through the window a goat tied to a post eating grass. The barracks stood on what had once been a pasture, but a formidable barbed-wire fence now divided the barracks from the remaining ten yards of grass.

This was my conversation, in French, with a naked young girl lying on the couch.

"How old are you?"

"Seventeen. I speak German, too." She smiled drearily.

"Oh, I love to speak your language. It is so beautiful. How did you get here?"

"My two brothers and my mother have been taken to German factories, and my father is in the French army. The last we heard about him from the Red Cross in Switzerland was that he was still alive. I did not want to leave my grandmother, but I was put here. Monsieur, hurry up. I'm not allowed . . ."

"How many men do you have a day?"

"It depends—sometimes twenty, sometimes forty," she muttered.

"Do you get for each of them the two marks we pay at the entrance?"

"We get stamps for food, and we are not allowed to use German money. We have occupation money."

"I'm sorry I cannot stay. I will miss my train. It's later than I thought." I left.

The whole bunker screamed. "What a fool you are, Hermanns!" And many coarse jokes were fired at me and some on their bunks made a live demonstration of how they would have done it. In the commotion, Soldier First Class Brandt, who had looked into my other papers, had a moral impulse. "You don't know how near your last hour will be!" he exclaimed. He asked me to read more of what I had written.

I proceeded with events aboard the train into Germany. I had again been crammed into a compartment with other men on leave. The train was slow and had to make a detour because the Luxembourg area had been bombed by the British. In

Charleville, the headquarters of the Crown Prince, a master
sergeant boarded the train followed by a soldier with his eyes
bandaged. When no one stood up for the master sergeant, I
felt uneasy. My neighbor, a rather witty man from Cologne
named Pete, touched his beard and said, "I would rather have
my beard shaved off than bother to stand up for that fat belly
who has never seen the front. Men like him spend their time in
the rear writing letters to the wives of men who fall in action."
And, loud enough for the master sergeant to hear, he added, "I
was at Verdun, and will offer my seat to no one. I have well
deserved it."

The master sergeant, who had a wedding band on his finger,
became red under his collar and shouted, "I command you to
give me your seat—get up!" I was flabbergasted to see the man
from Cologne get up, give up his seat, and peevishly stand,
looking out the window. Turning to the rest of us, the sergeant
shouted, "If there is any more insubordination, I will send you
all to the last wagon at our next stop. The field gendarmes will
take care of you!"

He handed the blind soldier a piece of chocolate and gave
him some coffee from his canteen. The sergeant had a big blond
mustache like that of the Kaiser and my father. This gave me a
feeling of familiarity with him. "This man was at Verdun, too,"
he said to me, "and was blinded by a gas shell thrown into his
shelter at Douaumont. He is now on his way to an eye clinic in
Brussels."

The master sergeant fell asleep, and was soon snoring. Pete
turned to us. "Has anybody got a match? Put it under his nose;
it will explode." Then he said to me: "Comrade of Koblenz,
what do you say, shall we get hold of his belt sack? We might
find some schnapps and more chocolate there."

"You do nothing of the sort," snapped the blind man, "or I'll
wake him up."

"But we will share it with you," said Pete. "I won't take it for myself, but for my children at home who are starving. Those *Etappenschweine* [rear pigs] have fattened themselves with the cheese and iron rations which never reached us in the *Scheisse* at Verdun. You were at Verdun, too, weren't you?"

"Yes, and I was a volunteer." There was a momentary silence as tears appeared from underneath the bandage and slowly trickled to his mouth. He was perhaps eighteen. "What will my mother say when she sees me?" he said. He sat opposite me, so I took his hand and held it awhile.

"Do you want a drink?" I asked. "Maybe a little one?"

"No," he said, "I need to take a leak."

Since there was no toilet in the place, we looked for any empty can. Someone opened his iron ration and ate it hastily— it was supposed to keep him going until he reached Hanover, some ten hours away—then handed the can to the young man. We had to empty it out the window several times.

At Liège, the train stopped and a sergeant from another compartment opened the door and yelled our master sergeant out of his sleep. I helped him assist the blind man from the train, and used that opportunity to look around. Even though the station was pitch black, I noticed a sad procession of blindfolded soldiers coming from several compartments of the train. The name Verdun became carved in my heart.

And now, as the train rolled on toward Cologne, we men began to unburden our hearts. One soldier said he had been sick with dysentery and had been hospitalized at Avricourt, where the Kaiser's second son had his headquarters in a nearby castle. He then told us details of the carousing going on there, and ended with, "It will burn one day, like Sodom and Gomorrah."

Another soldier said, "God was with us when we killed every man in Belgium who carried a gun." He then showed us a large coin made of aluminum. On the top of the coin was a bearded face representing God emerging from among clouds, and beneath it these words engraved over a mighty flame: *"Schlagt ihn tot! Das Weltgericht fragt euch nach den Gründen nicht."* ("Strike him dead! The Day of Judgment will not ask your reasons.") I looked at the coin and thought that if God was so fatherly that he could be portrayed with a long beard, how could he have ever permitted the young volunteer I had just met to become blinded by poisoned gas? I asked the others what they thought of God. All were silent except for two, who assumed God to be on the side of the Germans, since we had occupied a large portion of Russia as well as France, the oil-fields of the Balkans were ours, and the U-boat warfare was stranding the British. I became aroused and asked them whether God was also allowing poison gas to be used at our offensive at Ypres, and had allowed the *Lusitania* to be sunk. To my amazement, a sergeant who had been at Ypres said that these new *Kampfmittel* (weapons) were the marvelous invention of the German mind, for he had witnessed, when marching after the wave of poison gas had cleared, that all the dead looked peaceful, and that it must have been a quick death, without pain.

"Comrade, that 'peaceful death' is not true." A young sergeant in a tailor-made uniform, with a bulging black leather briefcase clamped between his knees, stared intently at us. "In our headquarters, diaries and letters of German soldiers have been copied for the Crown Prince. They tell a different story. Some staff officers wanted to have those diaries and reports published in neutral countries in order to frighten France and England into surrender, but the Crown Prince and several generals thought it better to destroy the evidence, since his father, the Kaiser, had already been called 'William the Poisoner,' even in American newspapers."

I had been so absorbed with the tale of my furlough experiences that I was not aware that an ominous quiet had spread throughout the bunker like an imagined cloud of poison gas.

"Let's not have any more about gas warfare," one man said quietly. "*Miesmacher* [Defeatist]!" came a cry from the back. "Lies! All of it must be lies!"

A few men wanted me to continue. Yet I felt as though I had fallen into a trap caused by the very freedom of my pen. "Don't be downhearted," I said, smiling a little. "Here is a speech I heard a general give, just yesterday on a platform in Charleville. 'You come from home and have seen less food than you had expected, and you have also read newspapers like the one I hold in my hand with the headline "WHY ARE WE GERMANS SO HATED?" Some will say because we marched into Belgium, others because we shot the nurse Edith Cavell, and still others because we sank the *Lusitania*. I say, be glad that you are not loved! Wasn't Christ hated, too? Remember what Bismarck said: "May they hate us as long as they fear us!" Remember: Decisions are not made at conference tables, but with blood and iron. This will be our motto: Keep your swords sharp, keep them two-edged. One edge for the east, the other for the west.' "

The bombardment had finished and some men left the bunker; others turned over to sleep, gloomy looks on their faces. My friend Hilgers turned his gaze to me, and shook his head slowly.

The very next morning, Master Sergeant Hoehne practically kicked me out of my bunk and summoned me with him to a deserted area. I stood at attention as he quietly assailed me, that cryptic smile etched on his face.

"Captain Hoepner and Lieutenant Langenkamp have no need for *Miesmachers* in their company. We shall see to it that your memories will not reach further into the company, or into enemy hands. It would be best if your diary was seen no more."

After consulting with Hilgers, I burned my diary for all to

see. I had an awkward feeling doing so, wondering how it was that the truth was so dangerous during wartime. As the dark ashes scattered in the Argonne, I did not despair. Most of its contents were safely in the hands of my sister Gretel, partly copied while on furlough at home and partly sent off to her in letters.

My cooperation eased the tension between some of the men and me. Despite this, I was not sure what threats lurked behind the cryptic smile of the *Spiess*. One thing I was sure of was that the military mind grinds slowly but thoroughly.

Luck seemed to be on the side of us seven furloughers. We had only two more days in the trenches before a rest period of fourteen days. The company was pulled back farther to the rear than ever, to the little town of Grandpré, where the houses were still intact. We felt like human beings once more. We could take warm showers and delouse ourselves. Strolling through the streets, one could hardly imagine there had been a war there except for the many closed shops and the absence of male inhabitants. Mostly elderly women remained.

With Hilgers, I went to visit an old church and heard from the priest that Grandpré had seen great fighting in the last thousand years as a gateway to the Argonne Forest and the back door of Verdun. Then he said something that stirred us: "In the French Revolution, the Argonne Forest was called the Thermopylae of France, and, as Leonidas defended the pass of Thermopylae against the Persians, so General Dumouriez defended the sacred soil of France against *you* Germans."

When I said that a hundred and twenty-five years ago I was not yet alive, he answered, "No, they are not the same soldiers, but it is the same doom. You wanted to force a king upon the French people—and they defeated you here in the Argonne Forest. Now you try to force upon the French people the annexation of part of our country, saying that we are a syphilitic and degenerate nation, and, since our birth rate is so low, we have no right to hold all this land. But in this war Joffre will defeat you. After Napoleon defeated you, he made a mistake. He didn't dissolve the kingdom of Prussia by dividing it up. That was the curse of Germany. Prussia became the center of the Reich, the barbaric east. Authority maintained by tall soldiers was her cultural achievement. If it hadn't been for the Russian Czar's pleading, Napoleon would have obliterated it from the map." He looked at Hilgers and me. "The Prussian sword was so strong that it Prussianized Germany. You didn't have one philosopher who rose against it to try to Germanize Prussia. Why not?"

"We Catholics in the west were in the minority," Hilgers ventured. I said that I learned in school that we were the chosen people, and Jews, Catholics, and Protestants believed this.

"That's just it," cried the old priest. "Even the Catholic priests were first German before they were priests. You all believed in the 'German mission,' as your proverb goes." And to our amazement he quoted, in faultless German: "And willst thou not be my brother, I shall smash thy skull!" He continued, "Louis XIV also had a mission. So had Napoleon: an enlightened and united Europe. Look at the laws Napoleon brought with him. You Germans are a tragic people. You want to conjure up Barbarossa, and you wait for the ravens to wake him up from his Kyffhäuser sleep. You dream of the return of the Middle Ages. You want to install the Thousand-Year Reich. This has always been in the head of those who rule you. And if you fail, you have philosophers to tell you that it is a part of Germany's destiny. But the next generation will achieve it. Your Moltke read the Bible every evening when he went to bed, but it did not hinder his applause of Bismarck's forgery of the Ems telegram. And when then the desired war with France came, he wanted to keep half of France and obliterate Paris. Yes, he read the Bible all right."

He smiled sarcastically. "I guess the pages were torn out where Isaiah speaks of changing swords into plowshares. Or maybe he has read it and thought with Prussian thoroughness that since Prussian weapons are not mentioned, then Prussia is exempt. He probably also thought that the words 'He who takes up the sword shall perish by the sword' applies to us degenerate French, but exempts the chosen people.

"We shall not make any peace with your Kaiser until he loses his throne. We are now going to Verdun, my friends." I felt my heart pound. How did he know?

This old gray-haired priest with angry brown eyes then led us to the statue of St. Joan of Arc inside the church. "She is our saint now, the patroness of France, the eldest daughter of the Church. She once threw the British from our sacred soil; she is now in our hearts to inspire us to throw you from France."

A strange thing then happened. He blessed Hilgers, who kneeled before the statue and said the rosary. I could not help asking Hilgers on our way out whether he wanted to persuade Joan of Arc to change sides.

"Don't be facetious, Willie, it isn't your nature."

"But the war has changed my nature." I grabbed his arm. "Look at me and tell me what you prayed for . . . for German victory?"

He sat down on the doorstep of the priest's house. "Willie, I prayed for my soul. I had a premonition that I'll not come back. My poor mother, I'm her only hope, and she thought to have a priest in the family would help her into the next life." He laughed bitterly. "And now she has to lay her son on the altar of the Fatherland."

He rose and we began to walk back to our quarters. He asked me whether I also felt that I wouldn't come back.

"No, I always felt I would remain alive to write—to live up to the vision of my aunt who saw me as a poet. And then, too,

58

THE HOLOCAUST

I'd like to make good, for I was such a disappointment to my father because of my bad grades."

"But the war will end this all for you, too, I'm afraid. Willie, you must pray for your soul."

"Have you talked to anybody in our company about this?"

"Believe me," he said with a melancholy gesture of resignation, "there are many who feel they are going to be slaughtered. But what can they do?"

That night Hilgers helped me reconstruct and write out the conversation with the priest.

During our time in Grandpré, we were given gas masks and chased through a gas-filled cellar to find out whether they fitted properly. For those who wore spectacles, as I did, it was not too easy. The temples of the glasses had to be removed and replaced with ribbons which were tied around the ears.

Soon that dreadful word made its way round among the troops —"Verdun." We were to go there and break the bloody stalemate which had, in half a year, extracted an enormous toll of carnage on both sides. Douaumont and Vaux had fallen, and we were said to be within a stone's throw from victory. All that remained was to storm the ridge of Fort Souville, behind which flowed the River Meuse with the coveted city of Verdun on the left bank. Photos were shown of the bald and churned-up hills around Verdun with the caption "Look! The fruit is ripe for us to pluck."

One of our last days in that village, among the few French inhabitants, I befriended an old peasant woman and her daughter-in-law. They had killed a goat, probably from fear that it would be requisitioned, and invited a few others and me to supper—to be paid, of course, with our occupation money, with which they could buy bread and other necessities. On the way there that late afternoon, my appetite was almost destroyed. Napiralla, one of the most fearless soldiers in the company, had been tied for hours to a tree in the marketplace, where everyone who passed from the regiment could see him. It was rumored he had stolen a beefsteak our lieutenant's orderly was preparing, had cooked it himself, and eaten it. The smell attracted two others, and though he bribed them to silence with a piece of meat, Napiralla's banquet was soon discovered. And now this poor Pole from Silesia had to atone publicly.

While we ate, I said to the old mother, who seemed to be afraid to look at us (she wore a deep bonnet which hid her face), "I feel so guilty to eat a piece of your last goat."

"Oh, monsieur," she said, "you are not one of the leaders. Why don't you fellows rise against them? I lost my son."

Then her daughter-in-law spoke up: "And her other son, my husband, I haven't heard from him in two months. We don't know where he is. Through the Red Cross in Switzerland, we learned he was at Verdun two months ago."

Then I let the words slip out: "We are going to Verdun. I wish I could meet him."

My friend Theodor poked me in the ribs. "You could be charged with treason for telling them where we are going."

"I don't care," I said to him. And then to the women, "I am from the Rhineland and I love you! I'm sure the Poles in our army love you, too."

The old mother went into her bedroom and came back with a little picture of St. Francis. On the back was written in French the famous prayer of St. Francis: "God, make me an instrument of Thy peace . . ."

IV. VOW ON A BATTLEFIELD

On the march to Verdun, someone whispered in my ear, "Willie, I know what you felt when you saw me at the tree. I ate the lieutenant's beefsteak and now I'll have his life, too. There will be plenty of chances at Verdun."

With that the picture of Captain von Kloesterlein emerged in my mind. Some months before, this battalion leader of our regiment had said at an inspection of overcoats, "How filthy they look! You are all pigs! Of course, what else could you be? Man begins with the aristocratic officer." I had not heard this myself, but it had passed from battalion to battalion and become common knowledge among the soldiers. He was known to love alcohol, and may have been under its influence, for no reasonable officer would expect his men to have clean overcoats when they had just returned from four days and four nights in the trenches. It was in reference to von Kloesterlein that I first heard the whispered slogan "A bullet from the rear is just as good as a bullet from the front." Another picture emerged. On the night about a year before, when I found myself sitting with a stolen rifle at the grave of a soldier, I had wondered whether such a rifle could not be turned against our own superiors. My premonition had become true.

We marched with only our rifles over our shoulders—our knapsacks and blankets were in the baggage trucks—and yet I felt as if I carried a great weight. Remembering the burned villages we had passed through, the priest and peasants shot as hostages, the mother and two children staring at us with hatred —I couldn't help doubting that the cause for which I had volunteered was just. The papers reported victories in Russia, Rumania, and Turkey, but I was not at ease.

Somewhere near the village of Romagne, our regiment was drawn up in formation, and soon General von Mudra, wearing a simple soldier's tunic, followed by Colonel von Merkatz and half a dozen staff officers in shining uniforms, strutted by with a big stick in his hand. Each soldier snapped to attention as the general peered into his face with his eagle eyes above the sharp nose, trying to instill in each man the desire to be a hero. I felt gratitude welling up in me, and would have loved to touch his hand—"Thank you for having listened to a young lieutenant." The general's speech was supposedly a message from the Crown Prince. After a long appeal to German bravery and a reminder of our glorious military history, the speech ended with the sentence: "They shall recognize us once more—we the victors of Longwy!" His speech did not make much of an impression on us, though, since some soldiers who had been at Longwy said in the barracks that this was the first time they had heard that battle called a victory.

A short time later, we marched on the main road, which was flattened out on both sides into desolated fields and was rutted and packed by a daily procession of guns, cars, horses, and men, continually through winter and summer, cold, snow, rain, and heat.

Passing the little settlement of Ville, which was hidden

within the fringe of a dense forest, we saw a handful of soldiers, led by a captain, emerging slowly, one by one, from between the trees. The captain asked what company we were, and then suddenly he started to weep. Was he suffering from shell shock? Langenkamp, our lieutenant, with his cap rakishly over his left ear and with a cigarette in his mouth as usual, went over to him.

The captain said, "When I saw you coming, I thought of how I came six days ago on this same road with about one hundred men. Now look at those who are left!"

We looked as we passed them. There were about twenty men. They walked like living plaster statues. Their faces stared at us like those of shrunken mummies, and their eyes seemed so huge that one saw nothing but eyes. Those eyes, which had not seen sleep for four days and nights, portrayed the vision of death. They looked as empty as the torn-open windows of the muti-lated church in that little town of Ville. Was this the realization of the dream of glory that I had when I volunteered to march with the Kaiser through the Arc de Triomphe?

The next night, we spent in the middle of a forest called *Küchenschlucht* (Ravine of Kitchens), and it was there that the smile of Master Sergeant Hoehne lost its cryptic meaning for me. He called six names, mine among them, announcing, "You are transferred to the heavy machine-gun company of Regiment Sixty-seven." Who were the others? A blacksmith, a butcher, and three farmers—people who knew how to handle equipment, but, precisely, people who loved beer and trouble. They were seasoned soldiers, either active when war broke out or reserve, and had never been promoted, not even to first-class soldiers. I was the youngest and the greenest, but—probably in the eyes of the *Spiess*—good enough to die for the Fatherland. With a grieved heart, I said goodbye to the comrades who had come with me from the officers' training school—Heines, Hilgers, Kaufmann, Ingenhaag, and Geucke—and to the two Poles who had helped me dig trenches in the Argonne—Woysnitcheck and Borcz.

Apart from missing these men, I was glad to be leaving. I knew that a German bullet might be waiting for Lieutenant Langenkamp, but I could not tell him. Had he a suspicion? Napiralla had been transferred, but there were others whom the lieutenant might have more correctly called Communists, which I was in his eyes. Where human lives mean so little—it was said that within three months at Verdun we lost half a million men, dead, wounded, and missing—there is not much ado over who kills whom.

Life was better in the machine-gun company. Housed in spacious wooden barracks at the sides of the main road between Ville and Romagne, we were trained in our new jobs. Within a few weeks, I learned how to operate the heavy machine gun, reputedly the weapon most feared by the French. One day, Master Sergeant Schoenfeld, who had the war title of Officer Representative, asked me why I had never been promoted, even though, as he said, I had the "baton of a general" in my knapsack. He had looked up my record and noted that my conduct had been very good. He was also impressed by my education and recommended me for promotion. "There is such a lack of intelligent people at the front," he said, "that you have a good chance of becoming an officer soon." Three days later, I was promoted to private first class, with the assurance that future promotions would follow.

But this pleasant interlude in the barracks was cut short. Early in the morning of October 15, 1916, the sharp whistle of the master sergeant called us to order. He stepped before us, wearing high boots and holding a horsewhip—an emblem of his authority. "The company will march to Fort Douaumont. There it will receive ammunition and proceed to the front."

VOW ON A BATTLEFIELD

While packing my individual gear, I asked Vogel, the company shoemaker who helped me roll my blanket and canvas, to send my sister Gretel a little box containing my poems. "You will find it in the straw of my mattress. I feel that I shall not come back."

He answered, "If the Devil wanted you, he would have taken you long ago in the Argonne Forest where others lie." However, he agreed to hold the poems for me and send them to Gretel if I did not return. In gratitude, I gave him my weatherproof pants that a wealthy uncle had sent me. I told him, "I have a premonition that something will happen to me."

Marching to Fort Douaumont, we soon entered a wooded gorge cut by a meandering brook between high slopes and ridges. The road became narrow and sometimes steep. The brook had swollen over its banks with the October rain, and we had to keep our balance on stones and stumps which bore the marks of many a soldier's boot or hand.

The narrow gorge, ascending and descending, presently widened into a densely wooded valley, whose slopes held three or four rows of shelters, like prehistoric human dwellings carved into a mountain surface. We had arrived in *Fossesschlucht*, one of the great military depots installed by the German High Command behind the battlefront. Here we disbanded for the night. Old Hochscheid, a father of seven children who had been at the front since the war's outset, took me to the canteen, pulling from beneath his coat a wallet which hung on a chain around his neck. And he spent all his money on Stollwerk chocolate and red-beet marmalade (Mudra grease) to feed me and lift my morale.

Beside the canteen was another cabin, the post office. To my sister Gretel, I wrote a poem on a sheer strip of birch bark in which I described my plight:

THE HOLOCAUST

There is a whisper in the air:
You are the tree and the tree is you.
I stretched out my arms,
The tree stretched out its branches,
Arms and branches built a bridge and we met.
The sun came out and breathed a golden hue over us,
And the rain hung its glitter
Between each finger and each leaf.

There is a guttural sound in the air:
You are not the tree and the tree is not you.
Bullets punched holes through the air
And the tree and I had no more air to breathe.
The silver helmet of the moon was dyed black by poisoned winds,
The branches charred, each leaf shriveled
And hung on the limbs like torn spiderwebs.
My arms shrunk and hung at my sides like two singed stumps.

I wrote to my aunt and asked her not to send packages with
meats that she had the maids preserve, lying that the canteen
was filled with marvelous foods. I ended the letter, "You see,
Aunt Veronica, everything is done to keep our morale high."

The next morning, after a breakfast of hot coffee and a piece
of black bread with ersatz butter, we marched on. We soon
reached a rolling plain in which were embedded the ruins of
the village of Beaumont. Arriving at the edge of what had been
a forest but was now a desolate landscape of blackened tree
stumps, Lieutenant Peters instructed us to take a rest and eat a
portion of our field rations.

I laid my head on my pack and gazed at the remnants of a
house with stables and a granary in the rear. The monotonous
rumbling of distant guns almost lulled me to sleep. It was as
though the house began to come alive. A roof of red shingles
settled on the walls, the grass-green shutters straightened on

their hinges, the windows dressed themselves with white mull curtains, and from the meadow I heard the call of cows that wanted to be milked. Was there not an old servant on her knees scrubbing the sidewalk with soapy water and a big brush until the red bricks reflected the sunlight? Presently the upper part of a Dutch door opened, and a little woman leaned out to call, "Bella, come and eat. Soup is served." I plunged into good times of the past. I, too, ate some of the soup at a table covered with a huge white linen cloth, hand woven, a hundred years old, from the dowry of my grandmother. The monogrammed family silver, polished by generations of maids, glittered under the soft glow of the candlesticks shaped like angels. No one spoke above a whisper.

The commanding voice of the lieutenant cut the air: "Forward march!"

Before me, the house with the white curtains shrank into ruins. The green of the meadow turned to mud and briar. The air no longer echoed the gentle voice of Aunt Veronica calling, "Come and eat," but the noise of shouldering packs and tramping boots. There was also a continuous roar like a thunderstorm reverberating from beyond the slope which we presently descended.

At the foot of the slope stood Lieutentant Peters with his orderly to count his men. For the first time, I saw him wear that heavy steel helmet which seemed to make him one of us. The officer's cap which he, like all the young officers, used to draw so coquettishly over his ear, as though he were strutting in Berlin *Unter den Linden,* had disappeared into the pack of his orderly. When I passed him (I was the last man), he glanced at me as if to say, "A man who has the honor of belonging to those who may become German officers should be leading the platoon and not hanging behind."

I marched on without turning my head. He walked behind

me for a while with his orderly. Was he trying to hasten my pace, or did he want to talk with me? How I would have liked to speak with him, to unburden my mind, to tell him of my premonition of disaster. We were two young men with much in common, yet the different roles we played forbade us to converse as equals. So we plodded in silence toward the rumbling of the cannon.

We soon climbed to the top of the ravine, and before us a vast muddy plateau stretched out, strewn with munitions, boxes, cart wheels, water holes, and mounts, and here and there a tree stump. The far end was a barren rise like a camel's back magnified a hundred times—Fort Douaumont! This was our goal, as it meant some food and rest, but there still remained one more ravine to be crossed, which we were told was known as *Totenschlucht* (Gorge of Death).

We moved very slowly toward this final ravine in single file, using the shadows cast by the sinking sun as a shield and the hollowed surface as cover. The horizon was dotted with barrage balloons. Had they seen us? Four hundred yards ahead of me, Lieutenant Peters, map in hand, reached the ravine and disappeared. A flash and a dull sound came from deep within a wooded mountainside, perhaps five miles away. I had just time to throw myself on the ground; a shell landed about two hundred yards before me, throwing up a geyser of stones and dirt. No sooner had this shot been fired than a whole battery behind the wooded ridges plowed and pocketed the terrain with new craters and swirling dust. I ran for my life, plunging over the rim of the gorge into safety.

Climbing down the shrubby decline, I heard Lieutenant Peters from the depths of the ravine call the names of the men in the company, and I answered, "Here." I was still about two hundred yards from the bottom of the narrow valley when I

spotted a man cowering in a bush. It was Hochscheid. I asked
if he was wounded.

"No," he said, "but I cannot go forward any more. I didn't
answer the roll call. I'm forty years old and was forced into it.
I can't do it!"

"If Lieutenant Peters ever finds out about you, he will court-
martial you."

"Let him come and shoot me," he whispered. "I can't go on
any more."

Leaving him, I despondently followed the trodden path
through the valley, where I soon joined the other men. We said
little, trudging along for another hour. At last we reached the
shelters built into the rocky slope of a steep hill we called
Steilhang, the highest peak on which Fort Douaumont was
built.

Again roll was called and more men were missing. We received our first warm meal since we left the camp near Ville.
After we had eaten pea soup and *Blutwurst,* we were led to a
shelter where chicken wire was stretched in rows of three to
support our foul blankets.

It was still night when an *Unteroffizier,* advancing from bank
to bank, shined a flashlight in my face, slapped and awakened
me. Our company assembled around a mobile kitchen where
each man received a cup of weak coffee and a large piece of
Kommissbrot. We learned that we were to assist other companies that had alternately worked for several weeks to finish
a water conduit from a spring on the mountaintop to Fort
Douaumont.

This change of orders, which allowed us to stay in the rear
and to sleep in a shelter, comforted us. For a soldier in battle,
a day in the rear means an added day of life. There was some
whistling while the dark lines of soldiers, laden with pickaxes

and spades, moved toward the top of the rocky elevations. We found other companies already working there, and sergeants from the engineer corps busy measuring the ascent to the spring. The narrow road wound its way along the side of the cliff. And for protection from French shells, the conduit was being dug as close to the inside as possible.

While we were digging, a couple of workers boasted that they had found a narrow-gauge railroad near the entrance to Fort Douaumont, where soldiers were unloading small cars laden with huge wheel-shaped Swiss cheeses, sides of beef, numerous cases of French champagne, and two huge bathtubs. They had become ravenous at the sight of all these luxuries, and began wondering how they could steal some for themselves. While others were busy unloading, they tried to sneak a sack of cheese into a shell hole but in the process were caught. The *Unteroffizier* in command threatened to report them for stealing goods belonging to the Crown Prince. And the word spread like a fire out of control that the Crown Prince was coming to Fort Douaumont, and it was for his comfort that we were building the water conduit. We wondered, If he comes so far, would he go farther; would he visit the front? Someone tried to lift our spirits by singing:

> "Dry your tears, Louise,
> Wipe your eyes;
> In spite of what they say,
> A soldier never dies. . . ."

But no one joined and the singer gave up.

We worked in oppressive silence. Even the vulgar, obscene jokes, that soldier's opiate in time of stress, failed. This work had been going on night after night, probably for weeks, and we wondered why the French, with their observation balloons and airplanes, had not noticed the freshly dug earth all along the

side of the cliff. To be sure, the smell of scattered explosions lingered around us, but there seemed to be no concentrated attack on the conduit itself. The pipeline almost reached the fort, and when the remark was made that we were ready to bring up the Crown Prince's bathtubs, one of the supervising engineers, a staff sergeant, offered this rejoinder: "Let us hope they will be filled with water and not with blood. I know the French." We wondered why he should say this.

After three or four hours of dragging and laying pipes, we were ordered to collect our tools and return promptly to our quarters, because the pale glimmer of daylight began giving shape to Fort Souville, on a hilltop three miles away. Huddling close together in single file, we were walking along the small path in gradual descent back to our burrows in the ravine when a thunderous roar shattered the silence. Tree stumps, rocks, and human limbs flew through the air, and then smoke and dust. Wherever possible, men lay flat. Some hurled themselves into the water-conduit ditch.

A few minutes later, the monstrous shells returned. Since daylight would soon make us visible, we scrambled down the narrow path leading to the burrow-perforated hillside. Adding to our terror was the fact that these shelters were still far down the slope.

As we ran, the enemy had time to pinpoint the targets. At the entrance to the first burrow, a shell exploded, literally blowing to bits a cluster of soldiers who were entering the shelter, scattering pieces of their bodies over path and precipice. Every soldier who retained the use of his legs ran furiously down the path to the ravine's protection. I crept and ran, crept and ran, and suddenly, through the dust and smoke, spotted a blond head. Advancing nearer, I observed a soldier sitting on the edge of the path, his feet hanging over the cliff. As I passed him, I said, "Come along. Why are you sitting there?" I stopped. The head was familiar. It was Hans Brandt, a volunteer like me, who had just come back from furlough. I leaned over him. "Hans, what happened?"

"Willie, help me. I'm hit," he whispered weakly.

I saw half of his back torn open.

"*Sanitäter,*" I shouted for a medic, but no one stopped. From both his and my first-aid kits, I tore out bandage packages but to no avail. The hole was too large. I struggled to hold his head upright and balance his body while pulling him back onto the path. But he was too heavy for me and kept slumping back. Finally, he fell off the edge into the abyss below.

A short while later, I was huddling in a burrow which shook violently with each close hit. My comrades and I were shocked to learn from the stretcher-bearers and medics that ours was not the first attempt to lay the special conduit. According to their story, five hundred men had been working on this project for months. Each company on the way to the front had to stop here and supply the men. Whenever the conduit neared completion, the French fired heavy shells and destroyed it. Fresh companies, ignorant of the previous disasters, then filled the gap. We, like those before us, had been sent to rebuild what had been demolished. How high would the death toll have to go before Headquarters would stop the pipelaying? Had the Crown Prince divine rights? Had any of those seasoned soldiers who died under his command ever seen him?

The men began to tell stories about the Kaiser, the supreme war lord. A soldier who had just come back from furlough reported that the vaults and cellars of the Imperial Castle in Berlin had been filled with mountains of canned foods while his own family was starving. Moreover, a special train with the comforts of a mobile luxury hotel had been built for the Kaiser, with one car, his bathing car, constructed entirely of copper. Copper for the Kaiser's bathtub! My aunt had written me that all her copper pots, including her precious heirlooms, antique copper bread pans, had been requisitioned by the army—for bullets!

I, the Rhinelander, also had a story to relate. In the beginning of the war, in Koblenz, I saw French prisoners escorted over the Rhine Bridge to the Fortress Ehrenbreitstein. They wore red trousers, and the people were amused that France should send its soldiers as living targets against our troops that were so efficiently camouflaged in uniforms of earth gray. Women singing *"Deutschland über Alles"* accompanied these prisoners of war.

I watched a well-dressed woman shout in French to one of the prisoners, who was wearing patent-leather shoes, "You thought you'd dance into Germany, didn't you?"

Alas, none of our patriotic scoffers, I noted, had the insight to perceive that those poorly equipped soldiers seemed to testify that France went into the war unprepared. Rather, they preferred to echo the propagandists, who cited these ludicrous garments as proof of French degeneracy. Is this the war which the Kaiser said he had not desired, but which was thrust upon him by France? Are we going to win this war? For what are we fighting? Everybody in the shelter asked those questions on that bloody October morning in 1916.

Earlier, in 1915, I could not go to war soon enough. I felt that as long as I wore civilian clothes I must shun the daylight; I was beset with fear that I might miss my Kaiser's triumphant entry into France. In school I had learned the phrase *"Dulce et decorum est pro patria mori."* When I had tried to comfort my Aunt Rosalia with this motto, she retorted, "Don't you think it is better to live for the Fatherland than to die for it?" How I had despised her for this unpatriotic reaction! I had learned to chant in the army, "We wish to hate because we must hate; we wish to hate because we know how to hate. We love together; we hate together. We hate together our archfoe, England." I sowed hate and reaped hate. Even the children I passed in France would gaze at me with hatred in their eyes.

What had happened to our conscience? Why had not the conscience of us young men, suddenly pricked with the cruelty of war, risen up in rebellion as a young horse not yet used to the spur? Conscience is a religious conditioning, I thought. The churches had instilled in us pious faith in authority, thriving on such slogans as *"Vaterland, Heldentod, und Heimat"* ("Fatherland, Hero Death, and Homestead"). But none spoke of the value of human life, of human rights, of humanity as a whole. On our march to Verdun, the chaplain, referring to the toll that might be taken of our regiment, comforted us in his sermon: "Let us remember that the row of crosses you will see at Verdun and the obituaries read daily by the people at home announcing the hero death for Kaiser and Reich will make the choicest soil for the 'German oak' to grow." Seeing my colonel present with a dozen officers at this field sermon, I asked myself what would happen to a chaplain who built a sermon around the theme "He who takes up the sword . . ."

In spite of the agony we had just undergone laying the water pipes, an argument ensued between two factions. One said that we deserved to lose the war; the other maintained that we were fighting a just war—we had been encircled by the Entente and simply marched into Belgium before the French did. A picture of sheep came to my mind. Sheep, who preferred to be led to the slaughterhouse now by the Kaiser, their feeder, rather than to wait for the possibility of falling into the hands of Poincaré, a stranger. The sheep could have waited; perhaps the stranger was not hungry—or maybe even a vegetarian! Lying on the chicken-wire mattress listening to these soldiers, I felt as though I became human chicken wire myself. The death of Hans, followed by this kind of excuse for marching into Belgium, knocked all the spiritual substance out of me. I began to loathe everything, including myself. I could not go on now with the hypocritical practice of praying. I pulled out a small prayer book from my inside coat pocket and gave it to Wolfgang Hetz, a Bavarian comrade. Later, a doubt arose that I should part with a gift my good aunt had thought sacred and protective. I felt I had enough misery without challenging fate. When I told Wolfgang about my second thoughts, he called me a superstitious softy but returned the prayer book.

Exactly at midnight, our company gathered in one of the large shelters where an old staff sergeant checked the attendance. A few more were missing. He announced that we would march to an ammunition outpost called "M Werk," the subterranean stronghold of Thiaumont. From there we would proceed in darkness to the front near the village of Fleury to relieve the regiment of chasseurs.

The night was cold. Now and then, a star gleamed through a thin veil of white clouds. In single file, we moved up the path to the ridge of the hill. Before us lay a trench, only half deep enough to conceal a man if he stood erect, which ran across a plateau toward Thiaumont. Silently we trudged through the trench, making ourselves as small as possible. Whenever a tracer flared up, streaking through the sky like a shooting star, we squatted, cowering in this narrow walkway.

I kept to the rear, carrying, in addition to my pack, a huge iron box of machine-gun bullets. Occasionally, then more frequently, I shifted the box from one shoulder to the other. Travel in the trench created difficulties, for often the passage was blocked by earth heaps or pitted with shell holes. However, the farther we advanced, the faster the group proceeded. Yet I advanced more and more slowly until, finally, I stopped. It was as if something within me kept me from going on. With my eyes I tried to pierce the darkness, but could only recognize the shadow of the man in front of me, with his big back, disappearing around the corner of the trench. I tried three or four quick steps forward, but my legs refused to obey, as though acting with a mind of their own, knowing that doom lay ahead.

From far away I heard my name called. I answered, and waited. Was someone coming for me? What would I tell them when they arrived? The echo of shuffling boots gradually faded away. I was alone, for once by myself. A complete calm came over me. I leaned against the trench wall, removing the ammunition box from my shoulder, and rested.

I do not know how long I had been waiting when I heard footsteps. Soldiers with Red Cross armbands passed, carrying wounded men on stretchers to the rear. I felt my strength coming back, and resolved to act. But what should I do? Should I drag myself to the front with my ammunition box? Suddenly a unique, exalted feeling overcame me. No one was present to command me. I was free to decide for myself.

I decided to follow the stretcher-bearers. They descended the plateau, going back the way we had traveled. Yet should I continue with them to Douaumont? I was not wounded or sick; how could I face a doctor?

At last I arrived at the *Steilhang*. I walked along the path dug into the side of the hill where the night before we had worked on the water conduit. My eyes were drawn toward a boulder that could at any moment drop into the small canyon. I recognized that boulder. Bending over it, I peered into the canyon, but darkness prevented me from identifying more of the landscape. I sat down, my arm resting on the heavy ammunition box. When the first pale light burst through the clouds, I slowly distinguished a dark form halfway down the large gully. With the growing light I perceived the blond hair of Hans. He was half covered with stones and dirt, and a dark red stain flowed downward from his body. As I sat there on the rim of the path, the earth began to cave in. I jumped up and stepped back to safety. But I had to sit down again and gaze toward Hans. I thought I should join him—then it would be all over. An overwhelming feeling of despair gripped me only to be pierced suddenly by such disgust that I stood up and sent the ammunition box crashing down the ravine. I listened to the trembling until the echoes ended. I thought, I'm free! I'm free! I don't care what happens now. I made my way down the path to the first shelter I reached and crept inside. In the darkness, I searched for an empty cot but could only feel boots. I found a corner, lay down, and fell asleep.

When I awoke, I peered through the entrance at the sky. It was night. I must have slept for more than twelve hours. Suddenly it struck me that I had become a deserter. But I also knew there was still time to make good. The others might think that I had become lost in all the confusion, and though the cause might not be noble or good, I nonetheless had given my oath to defend the Fatherland and give my life for it. Had I not been taught when I joined the regiment "A soldier is not allowed to think"? I decided to rejoin my company without delay.

I crept outside and immediately smelled the odor of the shell that had killed so many in that same place the day before. I hastened to the spot where I had hurled the ammunition box. Peering over the top into the pitch-black ravine, I searched for the container. To find it, I risked stumbling over the body of Hans, and I felt I was not strong enough to see his blue eyes opened and staring at me, as though still crying for help. I returned to the shelter and hurriedly ate a piece of black bread by candlelight. I then fastened my pack, strapped my belt and revolver around me, and hung the gas mask over my shoulder. I ascended the path to reach the trench, then ran through the narrow passage until I passed the spot where my legs had failed me the night before. It became harder to find my way, as the trench was more and more broken by shell holes filled with water, and it was so dark that I often had to wait for the light of tracer flares to confirm whether or not I was in the trench.

At the moment when I believed I was completely lost, several detachments of stretcher-bearers passed me on their way to Thiaumont. I followed them, for Thiaumont, besides being our underground ammunition outpost, was also the advance gathering point for our company. Even the stretcher-bearers had a hard time finding the entrance, since the trench had been entirely leveled for the last part of the way, and the tracers revealed nothing but craters, here and there pieces of rifles, parts of litters or uniforms, and unexploded shells. Once we had to climb over a dead pony, beside him two torn sacks. We stumbled over loaves of bread and meat cans.

At last the sound of subdued voices helped us move in the right direction. The entrance was a mere hole in the scarred battlefield, and the silhouettes of cowering men constantly crawling in or out looked like huge ants in the dark. I descended an iron ladder some forty feet into the concrete cavern.

It was an enormous place crowded with many hundreds of soldiers. Some lay on bunks sleeping, snoring and moaning. Some cluttered the passages between the bunks, chatting or writing letters. Others sat or knelt in corners, packing or unpacking their belongings. Here a flashlight, there a candle, match, or cigarette dotted the dark with flickering islands of light, continually shifting in brightness. From this subterranean stronghold, a small patch of sky could be seen when one stood close to the iron ladder or looked through the shaft which contained the ventilator fans.

The shelter could have been a huge substation in Paris were it not for a hill of earth which oddly arose in the center. On this mound men were also crowded together, some lying and some sitting. Those who were standing almost touched the ceiling.

I recognized one of the men in this group, a huge man, as Corporal Schulze from our company, who told me that he also had lost contact and had arrived there an hour before. The rest of the company was at the front. He advised me to report immediately to Lieutenant Peters, who was resting in a hammock a few yards away. To be presentable, I combed my hair, but when I looked into my little steel mirror I did not know myself. My face was so spare and shrunken that I could see nothing but my eyes. I was covered with loam, a phantom like those soldiers and their captain I had seen as I marched to the front a few days before.

Lieutenant Peters was leaning out of his hammock to receive a portion of the battle ration which his orderly had cooked for him when I clicked my heels to stand at attention.

"Where have you been?" I said that the others went so fast that I could not keep up with the heavy ammunition box.

"Where is the box?"

"I lost it."

For a moment he looked me over. Then he leaned toward me. "A good soldier either comes back with his weapons or not at all. You're going immediately to the front." In his tired, youthful face, his dark eyes flashed with hostility, but before I had time to say "*Jawohl, Herr Leutnant*," he had turned away from me, sat back in his hammock, and resumed eating.

I returned to Corporal Schulze on the mound, and said that I was going that very night to meet my fate. I opened my knapsack to get something to eat, but a putrid smell spoiled what little appetite I had. Schulze told me that under this heap of earth many French soldiers were buried, having been killed by poison gas when we Germans captured this underground stronghold. The dirt had been shoveled in from above, as it was impossible to lift the dead Frenchmen out.

An hour later, Schulze and I, together with a few other men

who had gathered at M Werk, climbed the iron ladder into the dark to advance to the front. The trenches were no longer there, and the white ribbon of phosphorus that had marked the way was destroyed, so that we had to be guided by flaring tracers and our compasses.

Advancing on our bellies, we soon found soldiers cringing in shell holes waiting to be relieved. They were in great confusion, not knowing whether the shell holes to the right or left were German or French. With the utmost care, we crept through the little openings connecting one shell hole to another, hoping not to have an unpleasant surprise. At last we found our company and were directed to our group. Corporal Schulze immediately took command.

I learned that the group had arrived in this hole a short time before, having spent a full night creeping about, searching in vain for the men whom they were to relieve. Failing to find them, they had decided to settle down here. They had already bailed out the water and mud. With the first glimpse of morning, we filled a dozen bags with dirt to fortify the ridge of the shell hole for the machine gun. Suddenly one of the soldiers pointed toward the far slope of the hole. We were stunned with horror.

The pale head of a young man gazed upon us as if stuck in the wall. We investigated. He and his comrades had been buried alive by a shell. Being on top, he had tried to free himself, but his strength had failed. Was this the group which we should have relieved? We covered the head with earth and wondered.

Taking advantage of the last shadows of the dwindling night, we built a platform for the machine gun and leveled the earth before the muzzle in all directions in order to have a wider radius for shooting.

Now soldiers in the next crater warned us: "Stop your work.

When the sun comes up, the machine gun and all of you will be instantly destroyed. The least change in terrain will be noticed by the enemy."

I became aware of our position. Every flare hissing in the air to spread for a few seconds a ghostly glare over the landscape told our predicament. Before us a slope rose to the crest of a hill. There, a mile away, loomed Fort Souville. Our slightest move could be watched from those slopes, which, although torn by shells, were still wooded enough to give the enemy excellent cover for his guns. We were lying on terrain barren for miles, with no cover except what the precarious shell holes offered. The French could look into our shell holes and strafe them at will from the surrounding hills. Even the greenest soldier could see that this place was untenable. And there were no officers around to boost our morale by example. Leaders had become scarce. Since the terrible losses of fine officers during the offensive of 1914, they had been ordered not to expose themselves unnecessarily. Yet when the Crown Prince began his offensive, February 21, many who had been promoted in the meantime ignored this order. Officer Representative Schoenfeld had told me at the last roll call before marching to Verdun, "Hermanns, your chance to become an officer is at hand. We need people with brains. Show yourself in the best light so that you get good reports. You have leadership abilities. Look at Lieutenant Brandis. He almost single-handedly conquered Douaumont!" That man, indeed, lived in the heart of every soldier. It had later become known that Douaumont had no French garrison; however, Brandis's act was a rare feat of courage, since he did not know that the fort was empty. And with his handful of men he could well have marched into a deadly trap. Meanwhile, many a young officer, inspired by Brandis, had dashed forward in the numerous assaults to conquer the three miles from Douaumont to Verdun. But they did not find glory—not even a grave, to say nothing of their name on it. When I came to Verdun in October, staff sergeants and corporals in my front sector had been entrusted with the responsibilities of officers. Indeed, here was my chance! But I discovered that no leadership was necessary, since the soldier was restrained to one move only—from a spot he had to hold to an unknown spot in the next world. When in the growing daylight I dared to look over the brim of the shell hole, bullets whistled by. And there was no longer in my mind the question of how to gain officer's spurs quickly, but, rather, was there a reason to cling to this fatal spot?

I had learned from newspaper clippings my aunt had sent me that in the supreme headquarters of General von Falkenhayn, the Kaiser's Chief of Staff, the plan had been conceived to force the French to fight under conditions fatal to them. The words of General Ludendorff underscored this plan: "The Germans at Verdun are fighting a battle of attrition which will eat into the flesh of the French infantry like a gnawing ulcer." Thus each soldier had been thoroughly informed about and prepared for those prolonged attacks on Verdun.

First, our artillery was to shoot for several days; then a wave of storm troopers or scouts was to follow to test the terrain. If the destruction was not complete, the scouts would withdraw and more shells would be fired. If it was complete, waves of trench diggers, engineers, and men with liquid fire and bombs would follow, then the main body in single file. Another line would follow to fill the gaps in the waves, and finally the reserves would come, carrying ammunition, tools, and sandbags.

In our training camp, a major told us, "Remember Verdun is only three miles away from you. The Crown Prince has assembled fourteen hundred guns, and these on a small front of ten miles, among them guns which fire shells sixteen inches in diameter, the largest of the war. Only two French divisions are opposing you. Joffre tries to divert your attack by an offensive breakthrough on the Somme. He has stupidly dismantled most of the guns from the forts at Verdun for service there. Thus Verdun will fall in your lap like ripe fruit from a tree."

It must be a huge lap for the fruit to fall in. My division and, so we were told, forty others were trained, all to be sent into the assault. Since February the fight had gone on. And General von Mudra, during his final inspection in September, spoke of the last fort barring the way to Verdun. When it was conquered, we would be covered with unfading laurels. This, then, was the reason: we were sent here to take Fort Souville.

How I would have liked to repeat the words of the young officer in the Argonne to General von Mudra, "You have ordered a superhuman task for us."

The fort looked down so threateningly into every shell hole that none of us dared move, let alone fix the machine gun into position. We were lying in shell holes of strange gray slime, as though made of crushed stones or concrete. Could houses have been here? Was this once Fleury? To us Fleury was nothing more than a name on the map, yet when reading German newspapers one got the idea that Fleury was a place where German soldiers could find rest, shelter, and diversion. Even my brother, who was fighting in Russia, had asked me in a letter how the French girls looked around Verdun.

In this autumn of 1916, the countryside we saw had not a stone, a tree, or a single weed to remind us that once houses, meadows, and people had been there. Nothing remained of the landscape but holes of all sizes, which appeared as dark disk-shaped craters upon a dazzling sea of mud whenever the sun pierced the dense low-hanging clouds. And the day before, in M Werk, it was rumored that the General Staff no longer contemplated taking Verdun but, by means of token attacks, would force the French to be locked in with a million men in this sector. As a result, Joffre would not have enough men for his offensive at the Somme. The task of my division would be, by intermittent attacks, to gain the heights of Souville and Fleury.

When this tale flew from bunk to bunk in overcrowded M Werk, many gave sighs of relief: at last we pull out of hell! A wounded *Unteroffizier*, who was dying of tetanus, suddenly opened his eyes and yelled, "I shit on the laurels with the name Verdun. I'll go home without them." A young officer came dashing through the passage, stumbling over packs, munitions, and men, yelling, "Who said this, who said this? What—an *Unteroffizier!* What company? I want his name—his name!" From the vantage point of my mound, I could see him being led to a man shaking in cramps and covered with his tent cloth. I heard him say in a rather subdued tone to a soldier, "Why didn't you tell me?" and then watched him climb back through the throng.

While passing the long hours of the night in the shell hole with Schulze and two others of the machine-gun crew, Czib and Peter, I related the words of the dying man. Schulze hit me on the helmet, and it sank over my ears: "Keep that to yourself." Peter said, "I could well do it without laurels on my head, too."

"What kind of men do I have here?" snapped Schulze, giving each of us the *Unteroffizier* look. I asked Schulze quietly, "Would it not have been wiser for the General Staff to contemplate a withdrawal instead of token attacks—?" Schultz cut in, "The French must not think we have been beaten back; the world must never be allowed to believe the Germans were defeated at Verdun. Remember, we are inflicting a war of attrition on the enemy, bleeding the French white."

"Who is bleeding whom white?" I asked. "Fleury has been taken and retaken sixteen times in twenty-six days. Every gust of wind that sweeps through here brings the stench of the dead."

And what an answer I received. "Hermanns, and you wanted

to become an officer! You should be ashamed of yourself! Have you ever thought of what people at home would think if we give up this terrain, every inch paved with our dead?" He punched me in the ribs. "Wake up!" I retorted, "Yes, tomorrow your corpse and mine will be lying here, too!"

A voice with a Polish accent cut in. "Yes, our corpses, all for *Deutschland über alles!*" Schulze glanced at Czib, spit, and said, "Polack, shut up!" I looked to Schulze: "Remember, we are here to fight the French, not each other."

"And you should remember that the soldier's job is to obey, not philosophize."

I couldn't help saying, "Schulze, if I get out of here, I will make you a warning light for other generations. Your opinion is that we have to die here to keep up the morale at home. You opened my eyes! And I may tell you now that this war is not a war against the French, but against my conscience!"

"Conscience," he snapped. "What has that to do with this war? We have sworn an oath!"

"Wouldn't it be better to tell the people at home the truth?"

"What truth?" Schulze's eyes flashed threateningly.

"I'll tell you if you promise not to report me." Now the old Schulze reappeared with a paternal attitude, probably instilled by his being five years older and a head taller.

"Willie, you know I wouldn't harm you."

"All right, then, the truth is that we can't win this war. I'll tell you why. I have a stepmother—I don't care for her. She is a cold, unemotional Westphalian. But one thing she has implanted in me. She said, 'Nature has an inherent law of justice. And woe if we violate it!' Look at the ravage we did in France. The tears of the French mothers and—look at the agony we soldiers go through. Can't you feel the souls of the dead of Fleury around us? They are cursing you and me and the Kaiser!"

Schulze pulled away from me into the corner of the shell hole and after a pitiful glance said, "I'll report you. You have gone mad!"

Perhaps I had. In that moment, I felt on the verge of insanity. "Schulze, haven't you ever thought about it—what happens to a man who sits beside you and suddenly drops dead with a bullet through his heart? And what happens to him who fired this

bullet? There must be some wrong there which cannot be covered up with a prayer or a national flag! That wrong needs to be balanced somehow. It needs to be righted! We just can't go on killing, for we are interfering with the laws of life; nature will make us pay for it! You and me and the German people, because we invaded France!" I grabbed his hand. "Do you believe in God?"

"Certainly I do."

"I believe I'm going mad. Pray for me."

Czib glanced at me with his gray piercing eyes, smiled, and said, "I will." He pulled out his rosary and mumbled in Polish. Peter, our chief gunner, looked at me, too. "Oh, Hermanns, you are all right. You need a woman. I could use one myself!" Schulze, a devout Lutheran, gave Peter a furious glance. "You, a man with wife and children, shut your trap, you atheistic idiot!" Schulze patted my back. "Hermanns, leave the thinking to Hindenburg and Ludendorff, the heroes of Tannenberg. You know they are now our supreme commanders. Now all things will fall in line. And no retreat. Let them be our strategists and our consciences."

When he said the word "consciences," I wanted to scream so loud that Ludendorff and the Kaiser would hear me. "Schulze, you know what I would tell them: 'You say you will take over the responsibilities for my conscience? Suppose I'm hit with a bullet after having shot people whom I've never seen before. I don't know what my conscience is telling me when I'm dying. Perhaps what I've learned as a child, "Thou shalt not kill," would haunt me.' "

"Shut up," said Schulze. "No more words out of you!"

We sat there, huddled together in our shell hole, not daring to continue building the platform for our heavy machine gun. Nevertheless, we had to do something with the gun. Peter got the idea of digging a little tunnel beneath the parapet of the shell hole through which we could aim the barrel of the machine gun. This way we could fire without looking over the top or moving much dirt. In describing this plan, Peter must have become careless. For suddenly, while a flare illuminated the landscape, there was a thin, whistling sound and snap, and he sank back with a bullet hole in his forehead. I noted that it was a clean hole, as accurately placed as if fired by a sharpshooter in a gallery. This was the end for the man from Essen, the father of four children.

We looked at each other speechless. The bullet, which passed through his head, had hit the sandbag behind him, staining it with blood and brains. Schulze folded Peter's hands. "We three are left," I said. I looked at Czib. Czib asked me, "Shall I close his eyes?"

"Do that, Czib," I said.

How different we were! I had gone into the war with the dream of becoming an officer and returning with laurels on my head and medals on my chest. Schulze was already in the army when the war started, and even now, at Verdun, held unfalteringly loyal to his oath to the Kaiser and Reich. Czibulsky was drafted when the war broke out, as he put it, "for cannon fodder."

"Let us push him over the parapet into the next shell hole," Schulze said. I found it cruel to get rid of Peter so quickly. He was still warm, and Czib had not yet closed his eyes. They looked so hard and blue at us. Schulze, *Unteroffizier* from head to toe, said, "Peter has new boots. He had just returned from furlough. Why don't one of you pull them off and exchange them for your own? Let us see what he has in his pockets so we can send it back to his wife."

I couldn't move or touch him. "Next time, bring some gloves along, soft gentleman," sneered Schulze. While Schulze removed a watch, ring, and wallet, Czib closed his eyes. "Shall we wrap him up in a tent cloth?" I asked. "No time for that; let us lift him up slowly and push him into the next hole at the moment there are no flares," replied Schulze.

I took a last look at Peter's face. It was dirty and framed by an unshaven, gray shadow. With great difficulty, we had raised his heavy frame to the brim of our hole when two flares shot across the sky, forcing us to abandon him, and he tumbled down together with us into the mud at the bottom of our shelter.

"Maybe we'll have to wait until someone else joins him," said Schulze.

"Who knows, maybe it will be you!" I said. I felt bitter toward Schulze. And now I made a discovery: giant Schulze was superstitious. He pleaded, "Hermanns, don't say this! You are right. Let us wait a little; Peter is still warm."

So we three crouched there in the hole with Peter at our feet. I asked Schulze, "What's the Crown Prince doing now?"

Czib answered, in his Polish accent, "He's probably just getting up for his early morning bath!" I asked Schulze whether he thought the Crown Prince wanted to come as far as Douaumont. No answer. I insisted on having his opinion. "Do you think it right that we stay in this miserable place to be senselessly slaughtered just so the newspapers can announce once more that the French attacks have been repulsed?" Schulze stared at Peter and pretended not to hear me. "He really died a hero's death," he proclaimed. "Come, let us make a promise among the three of us in Peter's memory. If one of us dies, the others will write to his people and say that he died a hero's death, death with one quick bullet through the heart. There must be no mention of blood and brains and suffering. We owe that to our people's morale." With that, the three of us wrote down our addresses. I gave my Aunt Veronica's address to each of them. They both gave me their home addresses, but I noted that they did not exchange with each other. I knew why and felt sad. In the shell hole, there was an atmosphere of distrust against the Pole. I had always thought that common danger would level ranks—apparently not in the German army.

This night seemed to have no end. In war a soldier becomes so conscious of nature that he interprets each change as an omen for ill or for good. A predawn wind came up. I wet my finger and held it in the air. It came from the east—from Germany—filling our nostrils with the stench of putrefaction. Schulze urinated in his handkerchief and held it to his nose. "Better this than that," he said. Now a reddish glow began to infiltrate the dark gray clouds driven westward. What would this first day before Verdun bring? Date: October 21, 1916.

The morning hours dragged through the landscape. The hill-crests of the Meuse Valley, still covered with trees, came slowly into full view—even from our covered position. Naturally, then, those on the hilltops could see us, too, at least through spy-glasses. While we three were still sitting in the shell hole, crouching under our helmets, with our hands folded in memory of Peter, we were struck by a deafening roar. The hills in front of us and the mountains in the distance were spewing fire and brimstone upon us as if they had become volcanoes. The earth around us was moving like an ocean of crests and valleys, and we with it. This could be it, I thought, the last battle of the world, prophesied in the Bible: "Retribution has come!" "Let us prepare for the end," I said to Schulze.

While praying silently, I suddenly smiled. How strange, how mysterious the human mind is! As long as it can think, it clings to hope. When I remembered that Armageddon would engulf the whole of mankind, while Verdun engaged but a few nations, I felt all was not yet lost. Of course, my premonition that something terrible would happen to me was still there, but I now sensed that it would not be death.

Beside me cowered the huge Corporal Schulze, trying to hide his helmeted head behind my body. I crept beneath the corpse of Peter. Shell hole after shell hole gushed up its stones and bones only to rain them down again. I felt as though Peter's spirit had not yet left him and I said, "Peter, I didn't like you, and you knew it, because you told those filthy stories all the time. There was sadism in you—you wanted me to blush, but you were a good man and will not mind if I use your body to protect me. I want to get home, I must get home and try to tell them about your end and ask my aunt to help your children through school." Schulze, listening to my monologue, said: "Willie, you are and always will be a poet—even here *in der Scheisse.*"

I do not know how long I lay under Peter, but his body became stiff and heavy; my coat and face were smeared with his blood. When night fell, the burst of shells receded, but we were so deaf we could only give signs to each other. We were thirsty, and the water in the shell hole was mixed with Peter's blood. We decided to take the water from the machine-gun mantle and fill our canteens with it, but since the French might follow up their bombardment with an attack at dawn and we would need the machine gun, we took turns urinating into the water-cooled mantle.

We sat there waiting. In the light of a French flare, I looked at Czib, the Polish blacksmith. What an ideal face for a medieval monk if it were covered by a hood instead of a steel helmet! Then his thin, waxy face could have signified asceticism and his sharp gray eyes religious fanaticism. But fate decreed that this Czib was not sitting for Goya engaged in invoking the Inquisition, but was sitting before me. His passionate expression was not fed by religious fervor, but by a national ideal—he hated as only a proud Pole can hate. He hated the Kaiser, hated the Crown Prince, hated everything that was Prussian. At home, he and his family and neighbors could not forget that the land had been made Prussian only a few generations before. Czib had a special reason for hating. His father, a mason, had been forced with hundreds of others to carry bricks to build the palace of the Kaiser; he had been treated like a serf and died of consumption.

Beside Czib in the shell hole loomed another patriot, Schulze the Prussian. He, a farmer's son of the province of Brandenburg, was the healthy and large-boned product of a well-fed upbringing. I never saw a man with such an appetite. He would receive his weekly bacon and sausage package in spite of rationing and starvation at home. Fearlessly, he told me, he would bring up pet bulls and ride them into the meadow. He had a square, jagged face, large brown eyes, and dark, short-cropped hair. Even in the mud, his mind was so soldierly that he would crack any louse with delight: "Another Frenchman." He would wash his face in any puddle which he thought was clean. A few days before, at M Werk, he had shaved the hair off his body and held a candle to his chest to burn both hair and lice eggs off, remarking, "Clean I will live and clean I will die." I liked Schulze for his manly qualities, a born leader. And he liked me for my Rhenish wit. When at a beer party before Verdun, my comrades tried hard to get me drunk, heckling me, calling me "soft milk-faced product of a governess," Schulze with his broad shoulders pushed the drunks away, saying, "One good thing you have to say about Willie Hermanns: one is never bored in his company."

But what was in Schulze's mind now? If Czib hated the Prussians, so Schulze hated the Poles, and would never address them but with the derogatory word "Polack." And in the same manner, he would speak of the one or two Alsatians in our company as "Dreckwackes" ("filthy Wackes").

Schulze suddenly squatted down, unbuckling his trousers. "I've got to take a crap. Anyway, that body rot is getting to me." We both looked at Peter. He was still there, half buried in the mud—how could we forget? Our thoughts must have been as close together as our bodies.

A moment later, Schulze crept to Peter. "I have a better idea." He pulled off Peter's helmet, squatted down, did his business, and threw the helmet out of the hole. During the night,

Czib had said that it was wrong to use Peter's body as a bullet shield—now we used him again. I pulled the tent cloth from his eyes. The cold blue glare was still there. I tried closing them but the lids would not stay shut. I remarked that I had read somewhere that the eye retained the last picture it saw on the retina for some time after death. I looked toward Schulze. "I wonder what Peter saw last."

"Perhaps the Devil."

"Why?"

"Because he wanted a woman."

I touched Peter's waxen cheek—everything was cold. "I wonder whether his spirit is still hovering around us in this shell hole and listening to us."

"Have you read this, too? I have enough!" Schulze snapped, shaking his head.

"Come," I said as I began pulling Peter out of the mud, using all my strength, "let us get rid of him." The three of us wrapped him in his tent cloth and pushed him up over the parapet. When a French flare floated slowly through the sky a few minutes later, I saw one of Peter's arms projecting above the rim of a neighboring hole with the hand dangling. It was as if it were stretched against the heavens, accusing them of permitting a husband and father to be sacrificed—and for what!

Before us, the predawn of October 22 began slowly to give subtle shape to the hills of Fort Souville. All three of us were aware of the common danger when our position became more and more visible to the French. But there was another danger— intense thoughts hovering so heavily around us in the shell hole that one could almost dissect them with a surgeon's scalpel. I felt Schulze's silent monologue: "I know what you are up to, Czib. And you won't get there." Schulze's dark brown eyes glared whenever a phosphorescent flare glazed overhead. Emotions are contagious, so I began to resent Schulze. I knew as well as he what was in Czib's mind. He was waiting for an opportunity to surrender himself to the French, who in the Argonne had inundated our lines with leaflets encouraging the Poles to defect and join their newly founded Polish army. I knew I could not stop him, although he faced another danger, the French themselves. Indeed, I had given Czib some French lessons in our spare time. He remembered well the sentence in French: "I am a Pole, I am your friend, I am your prisoner." I refused, however, to teach him in French: "I hate the Prussians," not so much because he wore the uniform of a Prussian regiment but because the word "hate" itself had become repulsive to me. If Czib thought his hour had come, so I felt mine had, too. I was sitting between them, Schulze with his hand always close to his pistol. Instead of a barrier, I wanted to be a bridge and said, putting myself in the role of Czib, "If I should become a prisoner, I would tell the French, 'I just arrived in this sector and don't know anything about troop movements.' Don't you think so, Schulze? We have to prepare ourselves mentally and play stupid as they briefed us. Besides, the French know much more about us through the civilians in the occupied zone than we could ever tell them—so there is no danger of talking too much. Let's decide what we will say if we are captured. After all, it's better to go on living as prisoners than to be dead heroes on the battlefield."

They were silent. Thinking that I had sufficiently prepared Schulze, I came to the core of the matter. "You know, Schulze, we learned in M Werk that there were so many desertions that Ludendorff has ordered court-martial and death for all deserters."

"Yes, death," said Schulze, with an ominous look at Czib. "There are two Polish regiments fighting on our side against Russia."

"Yes," said Czib, "the Poles have been promised liberation

from Russia, but no Pole believes that Prussia will restore our sovereignty and give back Silesia after the war."

"Whom do you dislike more, the Russians or the Prussians?"

"Shut up, Hermanns."

"Schulze, we should know these things if we want to build a better future for all of us."

"Shut up! You are a soldier," said Schulze.

Czib was not to be intimidated. He glanced boldly at Schulze. "We Poles hate the Russians but at least we understand their language. We detest the Prussians—we are *Mist* [manure] to them."

"You *are Mist*. You can't be trusted," retorted Schulze.

I laid my hand on Schulze's shoulder to calm him. "If you are so eager to kill, why didn't you kill the two who lay in M Werk with bloated bellies? They said they had drunk water in the shell hole despite the putrified flesh lying in it. You turned to me and said: 'Yes, they were thirsty. Aren't we thirsty, too? No, they wanted to make it to a hospital.' Then you turned away. Wasn't that desertion, too?"

After an ominous silence, I looked at Czib, and around his lips drew the shade of a smile, as if to say, "Willie, I know you mean well." I looked at Schulze. His lips were pursed and his eyes were fixed on Souville. But I knew what he was thinking. My thoughts touched his thoughts as surely as my knees touched his limbs. Several minutes passed, and then the words "Yes, Willie, whether you like it or not, if this damn Polack makes a move toward the French, I'll kill him" hissed in my ear. Did Czib hear it? A sarcastic smile played across his face. The realization that Czib, knowing what Schulze had in store for him, might try to strike the first blow, hurled itself against me. Schulze treated him like *Mist*, too, true to tradition. He was an insult and a threat to Czib.

I sighed and said to myself, "God, don't let it happen. Save

Czib." How could I ever forget Czib? As we had approached Douaumont in single file, he had carried my ammunition box for a while, in addition to his own load. He always kept close to me and pulled me out several times when my boots got stuck in the deep mud. He was twenty-one years old and as skinny as he was strong. Now I was to serve as a dam between him and Schulze, whose hand remained close to his pistol. If the French broke loose, I wondered, would Schulze take care of Czib first?

While pondering this, I saw the dark hue of dawn changing slowly into the harsh brightness of a full morning. Moreover, a grayness began to cover the hills and a cold haze wove a mysterious shroud over the shell hole. It was as if nothing were alive around us. We said nothing, but fixed our eyes on the heights of Souville. We realized that there was something more important to watch than each other. Would the French, suddenly piercing this gray veil, stand before us in their pale horizon-blue uniforms? We listened. Schulze crept a yard forward. He placed his hand on the machine gun. The French were not coming yet. Instead, the blazing guns on the hill began once more re-echoing the roar of the previous day. A shell exploded in the hole in front of ours, destroying the muzzle of our machine gun. Had it not been for the sandbags and the protective shield of the machine gun, it might have taken the head off Schulze. He threw a scared look at me. "Let's not be superstitious," I said. But an even greater shock than the shell's near miss was its familiar sound, not to mention the direction of the air pressure. This shell had come from the rear. The performance of the first day had shown us that the French artillery was stronger than ours. We knew also from German newspapers sent to us from home that because of the needs on the Russian and Italian fronts, ammunition had to be rationed. Nonetheless, our artillery was returning the French fire, but some of the shells were falling short, almost on top of us. We three had the same thought.

The young soldier we had found staring at us with dead eyes may have been a victim of these same German cannons.

Schulze said, "Hermanns, creep back and look for someone who has a flare gun to signal that they're firing too short—and here, take these canteens and see if you can find water." I didn't want to go, but Schulze, always thinking in a military vein, said, "You know you have fallen out of favor with Lieutenant Peters. Now you can make good." He sugar-coated my dangerous mission. "I want to see you become *Herr Leutnant*; we need your humor. Then you will promote me to *Feldwebelleutnant* [master-sergeant-lieutenant], the highest rank I can get."

"I am not interested in promotions but in getting out of here alive."

"Right," said Czib. Of course, Czib was there, too. I whispered in Schulze's ear, "Something tells me I should not go." He understood and grasped my hand. "Goodbye, Willie, no more time for philosophy."

"What I feel, I didn't learn from books. I can't go unless you promise."

"It depends on him, not me."

I turned to Czib, "Remember, not all Germans are Prussians. I am from the Rhineland."

"I'll wait for you. I promise nothing will happen." Then, with a grin, "I'm still practicing: *'Pardon, je suis votre prisonnier.'* "

"What does he mean?" bellowed Schulze.

"I taught Czib what to say if the French come. We can't defend this place if they come."

"We still have hand grenades. We'll stay here, and you come back as quick as you can. I'm dying of thirst."

I had crept on my belly toward the rear through perhaps ten shell holes when a phantomlike shadow moved over the ground in front of me. It was a low-flying plane, strafing everything that moved. Because of the deafening roar of the bombardment, its engines could not be heard. The bullets shot up tiny geysers of dirt all around where I lay motionless. I felt as trapped as a mouse seeing an eagle circling overhead. Soon another plane came strafing, and then another. I lay there playing dead, then moved on. The planes returned, and, discovering a foxhole dug beneath a shell hole, I dived to get at least my head into it, but boots kicked me out. It was filled with soldiers. Over the sound of the guns, I implored the man in front (whose head was so completely covered by his helmet I could see nothing of his face but a red goatee) to press further inside so that I could take shelter there, at least until the planes had passed. Voices from within yelled, "Don't let that *Arschloch* block the opening! We have no air here." I tried to press myself into the entrance. The man with the goatee, a rosary in one hand, said, "We can't breathe with you there. If you don't go, I'll put a bullet in you." He drew his pistol. I felt that here was something like the Black Hole of Calcutta, and crept away.

I lay flat in another shell hole. After an hour the planes left. I staggered out of the pit as a fog that was almost a fine rain began to fall. I longed for the night, which would bring some respite in the bombardment. Then a shattering explosion threw me into a shell hole and covered me with dirt. I was numbed. On all sides, new pits were being opened and old ones closed by exploding shells. I raised my hand toward the sky, saying, "God, save me and I will serve You for the rest of my life!"

I waited. Gradually I discovered that I still had all my limbs and enough strength to crawl out. Sitting on top of what was almost my burial chamber, I recalled how, prompted by a dark premonition, I had given my poems to Vogel when orders came to march to the front. Now I was to realize once more that man does not live by logic alone, but is endowed with intuition, a kind of mysterious foreknowledge. Aimlessly I crept from hole to crater, from crater to hole. Each time I left a niche, a shell pounded into it, and when I reached a depression, it smelled as though a shell had just created it.

Night fell. The bombardment let up and the strafing airplanes vanished. Although there were no landmarks visible, a soldier develops a sixth sense of direction. I crept back on my belly until, through the haze, according to our briefing, I saw a slight elevation which might once have been the cemetery of the village of Fleury. I knew that the shell hole where I had left Schulze and Czib must be to my left. As I moved that way, my hand touched something warm. It was a leg that had been torn open and lay in a puddle of blood. I discovered a hand and face in the mud. I turned the head toward me. Bending close to it, I could just see in the dark that the face had a goatee, and I remembered the man with the rosary who kept me out of the hole with his pistol. Could this be the same man? Was this that same place and were all the others buried in the mud beneath him? Had my sense of direction failed me or had the surface of the terrain changed that much? But still there was that elevation on my right. I crawled some fifty yards ahead to the left of the elevation and whispered intermittently, "Schulze, Czib!" A flare went up in front of me. Had I gone too far? Was I in no man's land? I turned around and crawled back ten shell holes and lay there, watching the flare reflected in the water of a flooded crater. Earlier in the night, I had passed this large depression, which looked like a spring created by an explosion. Now I knew I was in the right area. I crawled toward it and took the canteens from my belt. Down low, close to the water, lay a soldier who had been shot in the abdomen. He whispered that he had been wounded two days before and had taken shelter there in the hope of being found by some stretcher-bearers, but none had passed that way. He had had no food and was too weak to drink. I filled the canteens and tried to get him to drink, but when I brought the canteen to his lips, he only pointed to his pistol. He wanted to be shot.

I sat beside him thinking that there was no God, for if there were, the very stones in the shell hole, crying out in compassion, would have moved Him to intercede. Yet a few hours earlier I had been praying. Could I really say my prayer had saved me? It wasn't over yet; perhaps I had just been lucky. Hadn't the bearded man said the rosary?

I promised the wounded soldier I would return with others, and carry him to the shelter of M Werk. In my heart, of course, I was certain that would never happen. Death would come first. I left him and crept on, certain now that I was in the right area. Suddenly I became frantic. Czib had said the rosary, too. "God!" I cried into the night, "don't let it happen—I'll believe in You. Give me that sign and I'll know You are there, and I'll serve You."

The night was cold. I was freezing and yet I felt sweat running down my forehead. At each shell hole, I stopped and whispered, "Czib, Schulze, are you there?" I listened, crept to the next, and whispered again.

When the first rays of the morning light haltingly moved over the battlefield, I discovered a man draped over the rim of two shell holes, with his boots hanging down into one, where I stopped, and his head in the other. There was something familiar about the form. I pulled the legs down into the hole, and when I saw the hand, I grabbed it. On one finger was the copper ring that Czibulsky had made from a shell casing. He had made it for me, but it was too big so he wore it himself on his little finger. I pulled the body farther into the hole with me, and then I saw that it had been shot just at the base of the neck. I wept.

As soon as it was fully light, the bombardment began again.

The same strafing airplanes flew low, a stone's throw above the battlefield, slowly and safely—for who would dare to fire at them and give away his position? The metallic "tack, tack, tack" of the planes' machine guns approached and then ebbed away. Thirst plagued me. I had already emptied the canteens and was trying to decide whether I should drink the muddy water in the hole. At noon there was a slight drizzle. I pulled off my steel helmet to catch enough rain to wet my tongue. While waiting for water to collect, I kept my head low, staying close to Czib's body. What a gruesome repetition, I thought, of yesterday with Peter.

There was a significant change: the shells were now exploding farther to the rear, as if the gunners knew that nobody could be alive in this area. The death zone had become no man's land. Were the French now ready to send in scouts? One could hear the incessant whistling as the shells flew over, like huge black birds, on the way to Douaumont and Vaux. German shells crossed by in the opposite direction. One could hear the endless dull booms as each shell left the cannon's mouth. The ears of us soldiers had become so attuned to these sounds that we knew exactly which size gun was being fired, whether it was a 150-mm, a 210-mm, or a lighter gun. Anxiously, I followed the hissing sound from the German hills, hoping that the curve of the shell would not break and the huge black bird would not fall short. Even more than that, I feared the French 75-mm shells, which whizzed over our heads in a flat trajectory. This was France's most murderous weapon—fiery forks of steel, raking the battlefield clean and leaving an impenetrable cloud of smoke in each newly made shell hole. I don't know how long I had been lying beside Czib when a discussion at M Werk about our fight for Verdun came to my mind. A staff sergeant said to a wounded friend that there was nothing else within this ten-mile perimeter of battlefield but wave after wave of assault and retreat, leaving fewer and fewer survivors after each assault, and more and more replacements, young and old— *Deutschlands letzte Hoffnung* (Germany's last hope). "When I come to the front again, I'll probably be commanding school kids. This is indeed the war of attrition, but not as the General Staff had planned." I was so shocked that while I helped pull the boots from the wounded man's legs, I dared to remark to the young staff sergeant, "So this is the war of attrition."

"Never mind," he said. "Get rid of his boots and remember, if we have one more man alive than the other side, then we are the victors."

Thinking of this in the shell hole, my head close to the head of Czib so that his long brown hair touched my chin, I suddenly said aloud to him, "If we Germans were to have that one survivor, how I wish it could have been you, Czib!"

I saw suddenly in my imagination how his handsome Slavic face, with its high cheekbones and piercing gray eyes, would be eaten by rats.

I don't know how long I slept. The helmet had collected more water. I licked it, put the helmet over my head, and made a cross on the forehead of Czib. I searched his pockets for his rosary but could find only a few sheets of letter paper, a pencil stub, and a billfold containing some photos. I found a tent roll on the rim of a crater and covered him, saying, "Czib, you were a good Catholic. Wherever you are, pray for me." It was about noon of October 23. What was I waiting for? With no living soul around, I began creeping back toward M Werk. Suddenly I heard a tremendous rumbling and felt the pressure of a huge shell roaring overhead toward Douaumont with the force of a flying locomotive. Seconds later, it exploded in the distance like an earthquake. It was bigger than any explosion I had ever heard or seen, and I wondered what it had hit. A few minutes later, another of these huge shells flew by and exploded with the same incredible roar. I hugged the ground, terrified, while five or six such explosions shook the earth. When the firing stopped, I continued making my way cautiously back to M Werk.

The thought that I might be confronted by Lieutenant Peters there once more and have to answer questions as to the whereabouts of my machine gun made me uncomfortable, but I had no alternative. I had to make contact with my outfit. I had nothing left but my steel helmet, revolver, and gas mask.

With the instinct of a bird, I must have kept my sense of direction, for I found the entrance instantly, although this time it was not betrayed by muffled voices. It now lay in ominous silence, while it had been busy as an anthill two days before.

No sooner had I put my foot on the first rung of the iron ladder within the shaft than a current of warm, stale air from forty feet beneath brought to my nostrils the sickening smell of first-aid medications. The survivors of a battlefield—what a picture! Every one of the chicken-wire berths was filled with mutilated, muddy, torn, and befouled uniforms. A dismal sight. There was a man with closed eyes, a blood-soaked bandage around his head. Another, beside him, lay twisting in pain. I saw some lice-ridden men who had scratched their bandages off to ease the itching.

The passages between the bunks were crowded. There must have been a thousand men there. Some had been relieved but could not withdraw to the rear, and some who had come to relieve the others could not proceed to the front line. All were imprisoned deep within the concrete and rock entrails of this German outpost at Thiaumont.

Lieutenant Peters was no longer there. I was informed that he had made a quick retreat to safety two nights before. He was not a coward, though. I had seen his courage when we were on the march a few days before and were suddenly dispersed in all directions by a bombardment. He was the first after the barrage to search through the shell holes and ravines for the wounded. But as an officer he had been given the opportunity to leave this doomed position, while we common soldiers had to stay on. Captain von Kloesterlein had not even got as far as Douaumont. The old story went from mouth to mouth that this captain had called his men pigs and said that only the aristocratic officer is a man. According to a corpsman, von Kloesterlein had reported himself sick, suffering from a slight concussion. Another corpsman mocked for all to hear, "Von Kloesterlein probably hypnotized a rock to fall on his head." Anyway, the captain, we learned, had been sent to the convalescent hospital at Stenay, where, as a staff sergeant said, "he will probably join the Crown Prince's 'brisk and jolly war' with the women."

I longed for sleep, but this revelation aroused me. I became aware that my golden image of a German officer had feet of clay. Would the enlisted man be the stone destined to smash the dream image of Nebuchadnezzar? For all I knew, the captain's injury may have been genuine and he certainly had never been a coward, but rumor had it that he feared a bullet in the back. And I had wanted to become an officer myself. As we waited in M Werk killing time with vented hate, I suddenly saw myself filled with something like *esprit de corps*. I said, "The officer and the soldier have one thing in common: the instinct for survival. If we enlisted men try, by any means, to get away from the front—especially a front so demoralizing— why shouldn't our officers do so? They are human, too. The instinct for survival knows neither class, tradition, nor respect. It knows only one thing: one's skin is closer than one's coat. Before we judge, let us make sure that we would have acted differently in the place of the judged man."

I ascended the fateful heap of earth in the middle of the cellar to see if I could discern a familiar face. I found one, that of Unteroffizier Firmenich, whom I had known as a boy. His large, dark eyes were still sparkling with humor, a typical Rhinelander. He shared with me a bit of battle rations and his last drink of water. I soon fell asleep, and dreamed of the little village of Neersen, in the Rhineland, where I once spent my vacation. There I met Firmenich and his brother, a priest. I dreamed of the old castle in Neersen, with its two burned-out towers and the big trees growing inside its roofless walls.

I slept for about sixteen hours, and probably would have slept longer had I not been awakened by a commotion. From the top of the mound where I had been sleeping, I looked down and saw a strange man standing at the foot of the ladder. His horizon-blue uniform, neatly wound puttees, and blue steel helmet were in striking contrast to our gray outfits. Everyone who could still use his legs crowded around him—the Frenchman.

He showed no strain or fatigue. His healthy cheeks bespoke good food. He had a revolver at his belt, a wineskin hanging over his left shoulder, and a little sack filled with hand grenades over the other. I asked him in French how he dared come in, and he answered with masterful calmness, "You and everyone else here are my prisoners."

One of the soldiers, a captain's orderly, led him to the rear of the cellar, where a closed section with field beds formed the headquarters of this outpost. Two officers were there, one of whom was a paunchy gray-haired captain with a small mustache. The Frenchman repeated that we were his prisoners. The officers understood but did not speak sufficient French, so the surrounding soldiers pushed me forward to interpret.

The Frenchman said, "I belong to the *nettoyeurs* [special assault troops], and was sent to this cellar to find out whether there were men alive here."

At this point, the captain interrupted with Prussian spirit. "Tell him we are very much alive, and will live to take Verdun."

The captain then asked his rank, and the Frenchman answered, "Sergeant," and added, "We have in the meanwhile occupied the heights of Fort Douaumont and Fort Vaux. You must surrender, for you are cut off."

He looked the captain in the eyes and continued, "We have brought up over a thousand guns, three hundred heavy cannons among them, to retake the forts around Verdun. Our artillery has been hammering your positions for days. Yesterday our big guns caved in Fort Douaumont." I translated for the captain, and added that I had witnessed the shelling of Douaumont and heard the tremendous crash and felt the earthquake—presumably when it caved in.

The captain snapped, "*Quatsch* [Garbage]! Tell the French-man that yesterday our troops broke the attack."

The Frenchman smiled and replied, "Yesterday we feigned an attack in order to make you reveal the position of your artillery. Then we destroyed them."

The captain ordered me to search him for papers. The Frenchman cooperated by putting his wallet and some letters on the table. Among other things, he carried an order from General Nivelle, which I translated: "An exceptionally heavy bombardment will overpower the German artillery and open the way for the assault troops."

The captain made no comment on this message which con-firmed the French sergeant's story. He had another order of the day, this one from General de Passaga. "Officers, noncom-missioned officers, and men: It is nearly eight months since our hated enemy, the Boche, tried to astonish the world by a thunderstroke in the capture of Verdun. The heroism of the *poilus* of France has barred his road and annihilated his best troops. Thanks to the splendors of Verdun, Russia has been able to inflict upon the enemy a bloody defeat and to take nearly 400,000 prisoners; thanks to the defenders of Verdun, England and France are beating the enemy every day upon the Somme, where they have already taken 60,000 prisoners. . . . The Boche is now trembling before our guns and bayonets; he feels that the hour of punishment is near. . . . We are going to wrest from the enemy a fragment of the soil where so many of our heroes lie in their shrouded glory. . . ."

The captain asked me to write out translations of these papers and bring them back to him along with the originals. Then I read the personal letters. From the addresses on his mail, I learned the sergeant's name was Jean Coiq, of Guil-vinec, Finistère. I translated a letter from his mother in which she complained of varicose veins from having to milk the cows and make hay, because all her sons were gone. She prayed for him morning and night. I thought of Aunt Veronica.

The captain, hearing the man was from Brittany, said, "No wonder he has blue eyes and blond hair, he is of German stock. He should know better than to fight against us. Victim of propaganda!" I wanted to ask the captain, "Aren't we?"

Had the captain felt my thought? He looked at me with scorn, then, irritated, turned to the soldiers—a dozen or more, who in curiosity had crowded to the entrance of his sanctuary—and said, "Go back to your bunks and do your duty!"

When the Frenchman saw that the interview was coming to an end, he again tried to convince the captain to surrender, assuring him that the French held the ground above.

The captain stiffened into taut military posture and looked around him as fiercely as he could with his sleepless, baggy, bloodshot eyes. "You are all witnesses to the constant inflow and outflow of men from this post, which is the best proof that we Germans control this terrain. This man is a liar! Hah! Surrender? *Was ein Quatsch!*" He concentrated his glare on me. "And you repeat every word to him!" This I did, but I left out the word "liar."

As I translated, I wondered why the captain was being such a bully. I knew he was tired, as we all were, but with a little tact, and with me as interpreter, he had a chance to learn the details of the French attack. Even if this Frenchman should prove that the image of Prussian invincibility stood on legs of clay, the captain, in the interest of his men, should be ready to swallow his pride and investigate the truth. If, as the Frenchman said, the whole terrain up to Douaumont had been taken, then we were only an island left to the mercy of the French, to be mopped up whenever they chose.

Whether the French sergeant felt the translation I gave was halfhearted, I don't know, but he continued smiling, unimpressed. "You have no alternative; why don't you go out and see for yourself? More than two thousand pieces of artillery have been shooting steadily for four days, and the German defense has been cleared."

With these words, he turned to leave as he had come, but the captain thundered, *"Alles Quatsch!"* Then, in bad French, *"Vous restez ici. Vous êtes prisonnier."* To two soldiers standing nearby, he said, "I make you personally responsible for this man. Disarm him."

The Frenchman was stripped of his revolver and hand grenades, as well as his wineskin, a piece of chocolate, and a slice of bread. Everybody grabbed for the food; such white bread had not been seen for years. Drinking from the leather wineskin proved difficult and sloppy, but the wine-spattered faces of those who tried provoked gleeful laughter. The Frenchman had to show each soldier how to catch the liquid stream while holding the wineskin away from his mouth.

Soon he was led into the corner where the first-aid facilities were located and the seriously wounded were awaiting evacuation during the night. Our young doctor, a tall, slender man with a warm Württemberg accent, welcomed him in fluent French and appointed him a stretcher-bearer. The Frenchman was not willing to change his role from captor to captive. He said, with a twinkle in his eye, "That poor doctor, little does he know what has been going on at the top of this hole, and it may well be that he will carry the stretcher to the surface and I will take the lead." I was amazed at his pride and confidence. I felt that I should share with him a piece of bread, since he had been relieved of his. When I offered it to him, he shook hands with me and said, *"Bon camarade,* but I don't want to eat it."

"Oh," I said, "you are spoiled."

"Yes, I am spoiled. We know that you have nothing to eat

but dry bread with some turnip marmalade and for you the war is lost. Economically, too, we know more about you than you do about yourselves."

My amazement grew when I learned that he was a theologian, and a Jesuit at that. He told me that Clemenceau had said that religion and the priesthood were not shelters for cowards. He explained, "We don't mind defending our soil and our homes."

"From us Boche," I added. He smiled. "That may be the right word to use."

"I am sorry that you were robbed of your good chocolate and bread."

"Ah," he said, "probably in a few days my mother will send me another package." He told me that he came from Brittany. His parents were farmers and his two older brothers had been killed in the war, one on the very day his first son was born. He had been killed at the battle of the Somme. The word "Somme" evoked in me the memory of my brother's last letter from the Russian front. I wondered what had happened to him since he wrote.

His younger brother, he added, was in the army when the war began. He was killed at the Belgian border when we broke through pushing toward the Marne. I thought of Cousin George, and of my Aunt Rosalia, his mother, walking from room to room in black crêpe, moaning, "If only he could come back, even without arms or legs! I would gladly carry him." I now wondered if this boy's mother would go through her rooms crying the same phrases. I felt weak and eased away from him.

On some sheets of thin white paper the captain had given me, I translated the Frenchman's battle order. Then, as though I were driven by some inner need, I scribbled down in an improvised shorthand some thoughts and occurrences of *Steil-*

hang and the field at Fort Douaumont. I wrote feverishly, as though I felt I would need these notes, along with the ones I had made in the back of my prayer book, at some future date.

It was about five o'clock now, and I wanted to eat. But as I started to open a ration can, I was distracted by a dull thud and an ensuing commotion. Suddenly I heard the cry "Poison gas!" I saw people around me putting on their gas masks. I adjusted mine, which still hung over my shoulder. There it was —a yellowish gas glimmering near the iron ladder. A gas bomb must have been thrown into the entrance shaft.

The cry "Gas masks on!" electrified the whole shelter. Soldiers ran to get their masks, which they had hung on the walls and in the corners or laid on their packs. Many who had lost theirs on the battlefield began to cough.

The wounded in the bunks tried to climb into the upper berths, while beneath the gas crept forward along its way, extinguishing one candle after another.

Soon many were dying, and the bunks and floors were filled with bodies over which the living stepped and stumbled in search of air. It was as if the souls of the dead Frenchmen who were gassed and lay under the very mound on which I was standing had demanded and were receiving their revenge. The alarm surged like a wave from bunk to bunk. Before long it had reached the farthest man, a hundred yards away. The panic was so great that I saw badly wounded men throw themselves onto the floor as though they wanted to drink in the gas, while others tore the masks from their neighbors' faces. Some had a reddish foam oozing from their mouths. I noticed a familiar face . . . Hochscheid. I wanted to go to him, but just then Unteroffizier Firmenich rushed up. "Willie," he said, "I've discovered a ventilator shaft!" No one else had thought of that; even the officers seemed to be unaware. "Come, let us climb up. Maybe we can save ourselves—and others."

We had to climb down the mound and wade through the gas. I hesitated to be embroiled in the life-and-death struggle for air, but Firmenich dragged me. I marveled at his acquaintance with the nooks and crannies of this death hole, and his ability amidst so much confusion to find such a narrow outlet.

When we arrived on the platform at the top of the ladder, we wildly turned the ventilating fan, sending life-giving air to the men below. At first it seemed I had no strength, yet I turned the fan for a long time. I could peek through the shaft hole as I labored, and I saw that the terrain in front of me was not being shelled. The shellbursts were still in the rear. It was a rolling barrage, and farther back toward Romagne I saw bundles of flames searing the air. Firmenich, gazing in that direction, called out, "Those are our *Drachen* balloons! Now our artillery has no eyes."

When we descended at last, we found the gas dissipated and the gas masks taken off. Many men were dead. The gas had been so intense that the buttons on my uniform and the ring on my finger had turned black. Firmenich said to me, "Remember, Willie, we must not hate the French for using gas. We used it first."

I went to the captain and reported to him that I believed what the Frenchman had said about our position was true, for I had seen with my own eyes that the barrage was to our rear. I said that the Frenchman probably belonged to the first attack wave following the creeping barrage.

The captain interrupted, calling me *"Miesmacher,"* and then shouted, "Get out of here, all of you!" I—and the twenty or so other soldiers who, driven by curiosity, had sneaked in after me—left the enclosed quarters of the two officers. What a tragedy that superiors, even when facing the same dangers as the soldiers, deem it beneath their dignity to show human reactions to a devastating truth.

Returning to the mound, I met Corporal Schulze. He embraced me, not believing his eyes. I shrank from him.

"What happened to Czibulsky?"

"Willie, let's not discuss this." He stared at the ground. "Our own lives are now at stake."

"You killed him!"

"My conscience is clear."

"Yes," I cried, "you can perhaps look into the eyes of the Kaiser, but can you look into the eyes of God?" Neither of us spoke for a while.

Then he stammered, "I don't know any more what we are fighting for. Can you tell me?"

"Yes, you are fighting for your promotion," I yelled. "I curse you! I shall curse you until I stop breathing! You're a murderer."

I was almost insane in my powerlessness. Sinking down, I threw aside my helmet and gas mask. I didn't care any more.

He had taken a step away from me, turning his back. Motionless, he stood there, tall, broad-shouldered, his head almost touching the ceiling, the perfect specimen for the Kaiser's Potsdam grenadiers. I wondered what he would do next. Would he shoot himself? I couldn't stand the sight of him. I looked away.

Suddenly I heard a moan, and then sobbing. I looked about. Had he stepped on one of the wounded lying around us on the mound? No. He had not moved. He still stood, feet apart, planted on the ground like an athlete, his hands in tight fists at his sides, but his head had sunk into his shoulders and his shoulders had begun to sag. His right arm lifted up to his face, as though to wipe away tears.

A picture emerged: Czib and Schulze sitting in a shell hole, each with his hand on his pistol. Each one had the urge to survive, and perhaps Czib was as eager to do away with Schulze as Schulze with him. Indeed, Schulze could well have been in greater danger than Czib. How could I judge Schulze? I wasn't there. One thing I knew: Schulze would live for Prussia and Czib for Poland. I had cried for Czib; now I felt like crying for Schulze.

I don't know how long I sat like this, but suddenly I felt a hand on my shoulder. He was sitting beside me. He whispered, "Willie, we must not give up now. I have a sweetheart at home and there are people waiting for you, too—your aunt, your sister Gretel, and your poems." He jumped up and shouted, "We've got to do something about it. We've got to get back alive! Willie, I'll help you get out of here!" He suddenly stammered, "You shouldn't have cursed me."

He sat down and I leaned my head against his shoulder. I couldn't say anything: I just wished I had never been born. Suddenly I smelled that Schulze's clothes were singed and I noticed that he was coughing. I took his hand and said, "I didn't curse you—my nerves did. Who am I to judge?" There we sat in two bodies but with one mind. We waited for dusk.

Descending the mound, we came across some machine guns and boxes of ammunition. Schulze said, "Let's not go back empty-handed." He took a box and gave me the less cumbersome machine gun to carry. "Remember, Willie, we want to make good. There may be few survivors from our company. This will look good and might even earn us the Iron Cross."

I looked around for Firmenich in hopes that he would come with us to safety, but he was nowhere to be found. He had probably fallen asleep in some dark corner.

When night closed in, we ascended the ladder. I carried the machine gun, and Schulze the box of bullets. "Out of here," said Schulze. "If we have to die, let us die in the open and not like rats poisoned in a hole."

I had never taken a breath so deeply as when I first got into the open air. The clouds hung low and full of rain. We walked from crater to crater, hardly able to see where we were stepping. For cover, we picked our way as far below the crests as we could without slipping into the dangerous mud in the lower depths. Some soldiers, having lost their balance and fallen headlong into the water holes, were caught in the mud beneath the water, and a struggle only proved more fatal, as if they were fighting against quicksand. There was no sound near us but the rattling of metal on our shoulders, the soft clicking of our gas masks, and the shuffling of our boots as we walked.

The terrain, no longer anything but shell holes, rose gradually to the hilltop of Fort Douaumont, which stood before us a mile away. Dark objects, large and small, protruded from the ground everywhere, but nothing moved except us. Corporal Schulze, with his long legs, was about sixty feet ahead of me. Now and then, I could just see his dark contour as he crept and walked through the thick veil of night.

Suddenly a shot rang out. I threw myself into a shell hole. I heard the voice of Schulze: "I'm hit!" I left the machine gun and jumped up to run toward him, but he called, "Hermanns, run! The French!" Before me several men grew out of the darkness, calling, "Camarade, camarade!"

Suspecting that they were storm troopers, the dreaded nettoyeurs, I did not wait for their meaning of the word "Camarade" but ran in the opposite direction. They ran after me for a short distance, then stopped and fired several volleys of bullets.

I ran, falling, leaping, and falling again, from crater to crater, not knowing where—just away from them. Suddenly I fell into a huge pit, the walls of which were nearly vertical. While I lay there in pitch dark catching my breath, I saw something white move in the far end of the crater. Something else moved with it, creeping forward like an enormous cat. The

whole crater now became alive. It looked as if big chunks of loam had detached themselves from the walls of the murky hole. Eight or ten huge men rose before me, one with a rifle pointed at my head. I was still in a half-kneeling position. I cried, *"Pardon, je suis votre prisonnier!"*

Somebody drew back the hand of the man with the gun, saying, *"Tiens, il parle Français."*

I remembered Firmenich's words, and stammered in French, "I don't hate you. I don't hate anyone." And then I collapsed.

The next thing I knew, someone was patting me on the back, giving me wine to drink, then pieces of chocolate and bread. He said, "Eat, *mon petit*. Don't be afraid. You speak French and will be sent to the colonel."

This man, who was probably a sergeant, chose two soldiers of enormous height to escort me. They took away my revolver and my belt with the copper eagle, and then pushed me over the rim of the crater. We walked in the direction of Fort Souville, the terrain which I knew so well; I had gazed upon it enough from my shell hole in the Thiaumont sector.

They stopped to search me. Soon they were having an argument about me, both hotly talking in a foreign tongue. By the light of a streaming flare, I caught a glimpse of my captors. They looked so different from the sergeant; they had dark faces. They wore khaki uniforms. Beneath each of their helmets was a red fez, and under that, covering all of the head except the face, was wound a white cloth, probably to protect the ears from the cold and rain. These cloths made their dark faces seem blacker and more frightening, for I had never before seen a black man, except in pictures. I realized they must be two of General Mangin's famous territorials, the Moroccan *tirailleurs*, Zouaves and Senegalese. We had been warned never to surrender or give quarter to these "depraved" men in khaki uniforms. During the last roll call before our regiment, the 67th, took over *die Totenzone*, the hotly disputed, blood-soaked sector between the forts of Douaumont and Souville, we were told that those soldiers who had milk faces should quickly grow beards. These territorials were the stoutest and most savage contingent Joffre had mustered for the defense of Verdun. We should aim our last bullets at them, and not be lured into surrendering by sweet words, chocolate, and wine, for in the end they had only a bullet waiting for us, and would gleefully take our ears for trophies. Lieutenant Peters had read to us a report of a May attack on Douaumont. The Senegalese had made a game of butchering the German soldiers who had surrendered, and afterward had danced about like "beasts from the virgin forests of Africa who had smelled blood."

I told myself that they could not hate me when there was no hate in me, and also that they were undoubtedly Moslems, and didn't seem half drunk, as sometimes were the French who "drank courage" before an attack. I remained calm and waited, and presently they came back. I had to show one, who had my copper-bladed knife, how to open and close it; and to show the other, who had my watch, how to wind it. After I had explained to them the value of the money they had taken from me, we marched on. A short distance later, they stopped to search me once again, discovering a few coins and a small prayer book in my hip pocket, a gift from my Aunt Veronica. They looked at it; however, when I mimicked an act of prayer, they gave it back. Fortunately, Czib's billfold, which I had stuffed along with my first-aid bandages in the inner lining of my jacket, escaped their notice. I was led into the darkness, always a few steps in front of them.

They stopped again while we were crossing a crater, and began to argue once more in their guttural language. I judged by their gestures that they were talking about me. Then I noticed on the bottom of the hole in which I stood a German helmet sticking out of the mud. I tightened. Was there a soldier, a young volunteer, beneath, perhaps milk-faced and beardless, an earless victim of sadistic abuse? My captors stood on the rim of the shell hole. The night was wrapped in a damp sheet of fog and it was as if I were looking at them through a gray glass; their gestures seemed unreal.

Several hundred yards away was the foxhole where the kind French sergeant had given me bread and chocolate and charged these two to lead me to the colonel. Would they obey? Now and then from the distant hills, an ominous light flashed through the night followed by a rumbling echo from the cannons. Instinctively I clutched my prayer book.

Presently one reached out for my hand and helped me from the hole. We marched on. Walking along the rims of the shell holes, we arrived at a system of trenches on the slope of a hill, and for the first time in days I walked on wooden planks.

We now ascended the slope to reach a fortified line of shell holes, probably the original line before Souville, from which the attack had been launched. We were shown the way to several officers, who were sitting on folding chairs in an enlarged pit where the trenches met. A canvas covered the hole. I was surprised to see officers sitting here with so little protection. They seemed to be in deep discussion and after a while took interest in us.

Now I learned the meaning of the quarrel between my two guards. When asked who had captured me, the taller African answered in bad French that he had trapped me and not killed me, because I spoke French. One of the officers took down his name. Both left, and I felt relieved, though the three officers before whom I stood were staring at me coldly. The youngest one, perhaps twenty-five, had blond hair, a round, red-cheeked face, and large blue eyes. He spoke German, the

German of an educated Alsatian. "Which regiment are you from?"

"The 116th Regiment." This, of course, was not true; we had been given special instructions for such an occasion, and to make deception possible, our shoulder insignia had been removed.

The Alsatian made some remarks to the two older officers, too quickly for me to understand. What he said apparently increased their hostility. He turned again to me. "The 116th Regiment is a Hessian regiment, is it not?"

"Yes."

"How long have you been on the front?"

"Four weeks; before, I was in Russia." They exchanged glances, and the second officer rose from his chair. For the moment, I had a feeling that it was all over and wondered what would come next. I had been seemingly kept alive as an interpreter; was my utilitarian service no longer required? I was scared. He must have noticed it; he pushed a little crate toward me to sit down, and the oldest officer, a colonel, with a mustache and forked beard, spoke to me kindly in French. "You are young and probably have a mother waiting for you. I sincerely advise you to speak the truth. Where were you captured?"

"At Thiaumont." They looked at each other and the colonel nodded.

"And the 116th Regiment was at Thiaumont?"

"Yes," I said weakly, feeling the tension mount. Wanting to show my good will, I volunteered that my regiment was probably ordered there to storm the hills of Fort Souville, which lay to our front. "We were told that Souville was the last obstacle before Verdun."

My effort was not appreciated, for while I spoke the colonel was conferring with his two aides. The Alsatian spread out a map of Verdun on the ground, turned on a flashlight which he dimmed with a piece of tent cloth, and asked me to point out the approaches to the line before Fort Souville.

When I had done so and the Alsatian had marked it on a map with tiny flags, the colonel said, "There must be another way. Every inch of this approach is covered with artillery."

I said I did not know of any other and eagerly showed on the map that I had come from Ville, stopped at Beaumont, then marched to Bois des Fosses, and from there to the *Steilhang*. The colonel looked at the others. "He means the ridge of Douaumont."

The Alsatian bent over closer to the map. "Yes, it's the ravine which leads to the fort." The colonel nodded. *"Allons."*

I felt that I had gained their confidence. "From the *Steilhang*, we went to M Werk—"

The Alsatian interrupted. "M Werk is a subterranean tunnel belonging to the Ouvrage de Thiaumont."

"Ah, where the Boches gassed our men!"—the colonel. It was as if I could smell the stench of the mound, and felt weak. A phrase hit me, *"Voilà un boche qui pleure."* The Alsatian's hand passed close by my face to wipe a tear from the map. I thought I would burst if I did not tell the colonel that this was not the first time I shed a tear; that I was human, too, not a Boche; that I didn't know better when I joined the army.

"Allons, allons"—the colonel again, and prompted the Alsatian to ask me about the tunnel. The Alsatian placed my finger on the map and with marked hostility asked me to point out the tunnel we used to come from Douaumont to Thiaumont. "We have information that there is a tunnel." He added, "Don't try to lie."

"I don't know of any other tunnel than at Thiaumont," I said, "which was our last stronghold and used as our munitions depot. We called it 'M Werk' for short. From there I went to the front."

"You mean you *crept* to the front"—the Alsatian.

"Yes."

There was a long heavy silence, broken at last by the Alsatian officer, who, prodded again by the colonel, asked me how food was able to reach us on the line if there were no tunnel. I said that none had reached us.

"You mean to say you haven't eaten for several days?"

I said that I had eaten almost nothing for four days. In our despair, I told him, we would eat in one day emergency rations intended to last four.

The third officer, a major, who had been taking notes, snapped, "The ponies you trained to bring food from the rear didn't work, did they?"

"I've heard of the ponies," I answered. "They were trained to lie down when their trainers did, but I saw only dead ones. We have suffered much from hunger and thirst."

This answer aroused all three.

"We know this," commented the colonel. "Last summer your Bavarian battalions mutinied at Fleury because there was no water."

A messenger entered with a paper. The colonel signed it, and smiled. *"On les aura."* ("We'll get them.") The major then left with the messenger.

The colonel continued, "Do you know where the Flying Circus of Richthofen is stationed?"

After some thinking, I said: "I don't remember exactly."

Then the Alsatian, in German: "Do you know Montmédy?"

"Yes, I passed through the town on the train once when I was going on furlough."

"When were you on furlough?"

"In July."

"*Voilà!*" exclaimed the Alsatian, addressing the colonel in French, and so distinctly that I could understand every word. "In July, he was in Russia, but in order to spend his furlough in Germany he had to pass through the French city of Montmédy."

The colonel rose and explained in French, "For your information, the 116th Regiment, with which you fought in Russia, was sent to the Western Front near Rheims."

I was stunned, for I had named my brother's regiment, which had been in Russia since 1915: I had heard no word from him for several months.

Now the Alsatian, looking straight into my eyes, thundered, "*Blagueur!* You are not from the 116th Regiment, but the 67th. You belong to the heavy machine-gun company of that regiment. Your captain is Herr Harnich, your colonel is Herr von Merkatz, and your general is Herr von Lochow."

The colonel stiffened. "And what rank did you have?"

I said I was a one-year soldier, first class. The Alsatian interjected, "A man privileged to become an officer!"

The colonel, stroking his forked beard, smiled to himself. "*On les aura.*" Then, sternly, "You came to attack Verdun, the heart of France, as your Crown Prince called it. Through these attacks, you wanted to keep a continuously bleeding wound on the body of the French army, but Verdun is invulnerable and will be your death wound. Your Kaiser shouted from the house-tops that this would be an affair of a few months. He underestimated us. He could not imagine that the French would recuperate from your surprise invasion and prepare for the war while fighting it. You shall see Verdun, but not as a conqueror. You shall pass the cathedral while marching to Souilly. There you will have time enough to think about your brutality, your crimes, and your treatment of French prisoners."

The interrogation was ended. I was led outside into a dead-end trench to wait. A guard with fixed bayonet stood beside me. I was so exhausted I sank against the side of the trench. I felt drained of my blood. The whole interrogation, with its barrage of words, lasted perhaps five minutes but to me it seemed a long agony.

What I had vaguely discerned before was now clear to me—Germany had lost the war. A scene of a few weeks past stirred my memory. I had walked with some comrades one Sunday afternoon from Ville to Romagne, when I saw immaculately dressed officers prancing finely groomed horses along the road. "Look at that officer in the uniform of the uhlans," a companion pointed out. "Just as in peacetime. And we are in the *Scheisse*, Hermanns. Mark my words—Germany has lost the war."

I couldn't help observing that the officers who had interrogated me, one even a colonel, were all covered with mud and filth in a shell hole, sharing the same discomforts as their men, and wearing the same uniforms, distinguished only by the number of plain stripes designating rank on their sleeves. Our regiment had never seen *our* colonel other than in shining new boots and a clean uniform adorned with gleaming medals.

I was so down and out that I did not notice that other prisoners had been herded together into the trench, and soon we were handed over to the guard detachment. It was still night when we were led away, strangely enough to the front again.

Soon we (about twenty Germans, and ten Frenchmen with a machine gun) stopped at the entrance of our outpost at Thiaumont, M Werk. Two Frenchmen, one with hand grenades, the other with a bomb, descended into the tunnel with a German prisoner who was to bring up the commanding officer.

Who came up but the captain whose answer to reason was

"*Quatsch!*" With him were a young bespectacled lieutenant about twenty years old and a handful of soldiers with hand grenades on their belts. The lieutenant translated into French the captain's statements that the commanding officer of this outpost was in Douaumont and that none of the officers now in the tunnel had the authority to surrender. No sooner was this spoken than the French sergeant gave a sign and his men took position around us with their machine gun. For a moment I was paralyzed. Did this captain, who a few hours ago had called the French prisoner a bluffer and me a defeatist, think he could avoid the responsibility for a decision by claiming he had no power to surrender? In one or two more precious minutes, the French would wait no longer.

Desperately I stared into the captain's eyes, trying to communicate my thoughts to him. How could it be, I wished to cry out to him, that after all you have seen you still do not recognize the handwriting on the wall? Twice within the last twelve hours you have seen it, sheltered where you were thirty meters beneath the earth: first, with the French sergeant who warned you, and then with the gas bomb that killed so many of your men. I saw the strain in the captain's face, as if he had been called out from a sound sleep. Nervously, he kept wetting his tiny gray mustache with his tongue. His gun belt hung loosely around his paunchy belly.

What a terrifying moment! Was there no one there to assess the situation for him and speak to the French? I looked around at my German comrades. Their faces were dull, drawn, and tired, as though they no longer cared. But I was not ready to be slaughtered like a lamb now after all I had been through. I did not want this German officer to decide whether I should live or die.

"Herr Hauptmann, please permit a volunteer who wanted to become an officer to state that Douaumont has already fallen;

our retreat is cut off. A few hours ago, I fled M Werk with Corporal Schulze to make it to Douaumont. He was hit with a bullet and I was captured. From what I have seen in the last few hours, we will die here in vain."

There was an ominous silence. The captain's face twitched; his bloodshot eyes pressed themselves out of their dark, bulging bags. His gray mustache went up and down with his lips as he searched for a reply. He grabbed his pistol and yelled at me: "You, you, I've had enough of you. You deserve to be shot! You're a traitor. In the bunker are some hundred men who want to fight." I stepped back, pressing myself cautiously between two other prisoners. "Do they really want to fight?" I cried. "I was among them. They want to live! When the gas attack came, those who had no gas masks tore them off of those who did!"

He stared at me in frustrated anger, and his arm lifted the pistol as he stepped forward. A voice from the rear rang out, *"Qu'est-ce qu'il veut?"* ("What does he want?") How strange, I thought, a machine gun behind me and a pistol before me! I stepped in front of the two Germans and imploringly said: "Herr Hauptmann, can you take it on your conscience to have us all killed? We up here will be shot and the sick and wounded below will be gas-bombed." I pointed my thumb back over my shoulder, and for the first time he seemed to become aware of the two Frenchmen kneeling behind their machine gun, waiting to mow us down at the slightest sign of trouble. The captain lifted his arm, and for a moment I thought he would shoot himself—but he only wiped his brow with his sleeve, as if trying to rub out the nightmare before him. I sensed that the agony I had gone through might well be his: the choice between loyalty and conscience.

How I would have liked to cry out to the world: How inhuman a uniform can make a man! With his muddled conception of honor, of dying for Kaiser and Reich, had he not thought of living for wife and child?

Behind me I could feel the French patience growing thin. *"Alors!"* cried the sergeant. I turned and saw him walking toward the machine gun.

Turning back to the captain, I yelled at the top of my voice, "Have you no conscience?"

The captain straightened up and, without deigning to glance at me, said to the lieutenant, "Tell them we surrender M Werk."

The French made me tell the captain to hand over his pistol and all the others to lay down their arms. Never before in my life had I felt so relieved. An amazing thing happened next. The tallest of the men whom the captain had hand-picked to escort him up the ladder, a man almost as old as the captain, probably a last reservist, grabbed my shoulder and said, "You've done it!"

"Why didn't *you* do it? You were closer to the captain than I."

"I don't speak French. . . ."

"No? But you do speak German and have the captain's ear," I fumed. They would have died rather than face the scorn of their captain. In a flash, the tragic figure of Immanuel Kant came to my mind. When the Prussian king ordered him to stop his lectures on peace and brotherhood, the philosopher destroyed his papers and wrote to the king that he remained His Majesty's ever-obedient servant.

EPILOGUE

We were sent to the prison camp at Souilly, a former meadow but now a terrain of foot-deep mud, with tents for the prisoners and barracks for the guards. It was closed in by a double row of barbed wire, with machine guns mounted on high scaffolds. For the first four nights, we had to stay in the rain, lying in the mud and covered by a piece of tent cloth, one for each four men. When tents were to be had, conditions were not much better. The rations of bread and canned meat were too much for the dying and not enough for the living. This camp was called *"camp de représailles de Verdun,"* and a very large poster in the compound, signed by the camp commander, stated frankly that this was meant to be a reprisal camp.

A medic who had been with me in the tunnel of Thiaumont gave me good reason for the Frenchman's hatred. He told me he had served as a doctor in a camp in East Prussia where thirty thousand Italians and French prisoners had been herded together. Most of the prisoners could not stand the cold and damp climate, and fell sick of Spanish grippe and pneumonia. Nevertheless, the commander of the camp had issued the order that regardless of the weather, all the sick must appear at the morning roll call as long as their temperatures were below 102 degrees. Within half a year, more than twenty thousand had died.

There was a "death row" made up of eighteen German prisoners lying beside each other in a tent on the straw, all stricken with dysentery. After three weeks in the camp, I joined their numbers, and every morning a young French sergeant would bring us a large can of black tea and unload his hate on me, since I understood French.

The handsome blue uniform was hanging over his skeleton-like frame to give his words the ring of truth: "Because of you, I had to build trenches to defend our soil, and I have caught consumption." How I would have liked to take his hand and say "Pardon me," because I felt guilty. Some seventeen months before, I wanted to be a hero and ride at the side of my Kaiser through the Arc de Triomphe. What memories!

One day I had stood before an elegant tailor's shop in Paderborn and stared through the display window at the lower body of a dummy dressed in shining brown leather knee boots and a pair of army officer's trousers, the thighs inlaid with pads of pig leather. Beholding this, I pictured myself attired in the riding pants and leather boots. I saw my upper body grow out of this torso, fitted with the rest of the uniform; silver, sparkling epaulets of a lieutenant on my shoulders, the whip grasped arrogantly in my hand, and perhaps a monocle in my eye. Before I realized, I had entered the shop to be met with a gentlemanly bow offered by the tailor in striped trousers and a black jacket. He must have studied me while I had been gazing at the clothing display, for in his hand dangled a measuring tape. He pointed toward the window: "Yes, these trousers and boots attracted you, but unfortunately they have been custom-made on special order by General von Brüsewitz for his nephew. My

EPILOGUE

tailors could make you the entire uniform within a few days."
Hastening behind a counter, he extracted several bolts of field-
gray cloth. "I assume you are in the officers' training school and
going into the field as an *offizieraspirant*?"

My head spun. I managed to reply, "General von Brüsewitz
is my commander. I just wanted to find out the price."

I left, crossed the square and gazed into a small water canal.
Splashing about was a grotesque horde of plump rats.

Now in Souilly, I realized that the glory of the officer's uniform of Paderborn had not followed me to the battlefield; but
the bloated rats had, the camp was full of them. And now I
was here, despised and smitten, among people who were gasp-
ing their final breaths.

The little prayer book from my Aunt Veronica had been my
talisman so far; I clutched it day and night. But doubts had
crept in. Was God a match for man's militarism? It is true that
God had saved me three times within twenty-four hours on the
battlefield: first, when a shellburst had half buried me and I
made a vow to God and was saved as if by a miracle; then,
when I was saved from poison gas in the subterranean stronghold of Thiaumont; again, when on my flight during the night
bullets hit my companion but spared me; and even a fourth
time, when the fierce dark-skinned storm troopers of French
Africa had captured me but left me alive, although in the open
battle there was no time for such pardon, no soldier to risk
leading a still-potential enemy to the rear of the weapon-strewn
battlefield.

Yet here I was lying on straw that would soon be used for
manure in French soil. Did God allow man's hope to be
quashed by the uniform? I had seen so many men die clutching
rosaries in their hands. Who was I to be spared?

But God was not dead.

One bitterly cold November morning, I saw some hundred

men, many with bandages, sticks, and canes, standing in rows in the big square of our camp. Each one received a round loaf of bread and a can of meat. I asked what it meant, and was told that they were sick or wounded soldiers who could not work and were being sent to Carpentras, in southern France near Avignon.

Hope spurred me on. I dragged myself to the infirmary, where a German *Unteroffizier* with a Red Cross band on his arm asked what I wanted. I could only whisper that I wanted to go with those men who were ready to leave the camp.

"That is just as impossible for you as for a hundred others who came to present their cases yesterday," he replied. I told him that I would surely die here in this camp within a few days.

"*Vögelchen* [little bird], go back to the tent you came from and take a rest. It is too late anyway; the list is full."

At that moment, I became aware of another room in the back, the door of which was open. A man was sitting at a table, writing. He had a long white beard, and wore a cap of red velvet with gold cord around the top.

The *Unteroffizier* said, "Go now!" but I didn't budge. I stood staring at the red-capped officer. Presently he looked up from his paper and called, "*Qu'est-ce qu'il veut?*"

Not waiting for the answer from the *Unteroffizier*, I ran forward into the room and cried out in French, "Monsieur, send me along with the others. I want to go where the sun is; I like the sunshine so much!"

He took off his spectacles, looked at me a moment, and then said to the sergeant, "Put him on the list, too!"

It was as if the gaze of that old doctor had given me new strength. He had replaced my lost status in uniform with a spiritual worth. I was no longer a number; I was a man again, a free man despite the "P.G." painted in white on the front and

back of my grass-green uniform. With a loaf of bread, a can of meat, and a blanket, and with a jubilating heart, I joined the wounded and diseased on the camp square. I visualized the sheets of paper which I had hidden in my bread bag as part of a future book. I had to ransom my vow. The cross of iron for which I had gone to war—and would indeed receive—I was not to pin on my breast. I would carry instead the cross of wood on my back.

With these thoughts, I soon found myself inside the cattle car moving away from that hell of Verdun and, with the increasing distance, from the reach of shells and bombs. Around me lay some twenty people, wounded or sick, mostly tubercular, huddled in their blankets. Some were moaning with each rocking and jerking motion of the train, and there was a constant moving, mostly creeping, toward the bucket which served as a latrine. Through some slits at the top of the car I could see far distant hills and trees gleaming with frost. Night came and I could see through the narrow slits those stars that had been hidden so long by the foggy dampness of Verdun. No doubt the train was heading south. I fell asleep.

When I awoke before dawn, the first thing I realized was that my traveling rations which I had placed under my head were gone. But I didn't care. When dawn arrived, I riveted my eyes on the slits to see the sun, and soon a ray found its way into the evil-smelling darkness. It was as though the radiant finger of some merciful being touched me. The finger became a hand and it seemed to touch my face. The sun had given my bones new life.

At noon that day, the train stopped in a huge dark hall, the station at Lyons. The doors were opened and we were led, carload by carload, to water faucets and toilets. On the track beside us was a long train filled with French refugees. I learned from our guards their villages had been shelled by "Big

Bertha." A young boy with a bandage around his head stood on
the step of his car incessantly shouting, "*Sale boche!*" As we
walked along the platform between the two trains, an old man
in underwear, a baggy soldier's overcoat, and a beret spat but
missed my face and cursed. I couldn't help pausing for a second, in spite of the cries of the two sentinels, "*Allons, allons,*"
to look into his white-bearded shriveled face. "I didn't want
this. I am innocent."

"You don't wash your hands in innocence, but in French
blood!" he shouted.

Coming back from the toilets, we all walked with heads
bowed, as far back from the refugee train as we could. Meanwhile the prisoners in the next car had to face the same
gauntlet. A young woman in slippers, on the arm of a Red Cross
nurse, walked a cat on a length of string. Under her fur coat
she seemed to be wearing a nightgown, and her long hair hung
raggedly down her back. The Red Cross nurse said to the
guard, "Poor thing . . . she has not seen her children since
they ran away from the shells. Now she has only her cat." One
woman held a gold-framed picture on her lap. Others had
bedsheets. A young boy sat on the sideboard of the train,
clutching a huge handmade inkwell.

I sat down in the cattle car with legs outstretched, not mind-
ing someone else's using them as a pillow, for I was busily
thinking up a letter to the Kaiser, first planned in Souilly.

The next morning about ten, the doors were rolled back.
Carpentras! We had arrived. I looked past the French guards
who stood by to keep us in while the soldiers who could not
walk were carried out on stretchers. What I saw, some miles
away, was a craggy snow-covered mountain, radiantly piercing
the sky. The sun was more brilliant than I had ever seen before.
I couldn't drink in enough of its rays. "My father-mother sun!"
I said jubilantly. I stared toward the mountain with its crest

looking down on us like a head with a snowy beard. It reminded me of the good doctor in the reprisal camp.

Even here, the ugliness of war surrounded us. We passed a poster depicting the Kaiser. It portrayed him wearing a splendid uniform, high boots, decorations on his breast, and his helmet flashing with a golden spike. He was sowing seeds in the form of human skulls, and underneath in blood-red paint: "The Kaiser, Your Master of Life and Death." I was reminded of the letter I had mentally composed in the cattle car. I hoped to find the opportunity to finish it.

As our ragged troop marched into the camp, I noticed German prisoners, incurably ill or wounded, waiting, we were told, for passage to Switzerland, where they would be exchanged for French prisoners of war. An idea occurred to me. When I had finished my letter to the Kaiser, one such prisoner might mail it for me in Switzerland, since a letter had to be posted in a neutral country if it was to go from France to Germany.

I was delirious with enthusiasm. I had indeed been saved, and now would begin living up to the vow I had made on the battlefield of Verdun. The letter to the Kaiser was the first task for my soul.

Souilly, France
November 10, 1916

Your Majesty:

Eighteen days ago, on the 24th of October, I made a vow to God on the battlefield of Verdun, while digging myself out from bomb-scattered earth, that if He should save me, I would devote the rest of my life to Him. Three times that day I was saved: in the afternoon, from an engulfing gas attack which suffocated many comrades; in the evening, from a volley of bullets on my flight to Douaumont which felled my companion but not me; and in the night, when the French, although under orders to take no prisoners, captured me and led me unscathed to the rear.

EPILOGUE

Now in their prison camp at Souilly, I learned from a report circulated by the French that on the 17th of October, Your Majesty visited your son, the Crown Prince and Commander-in-Chief of the Fifth Army, to try to discover an honorable way out of the discouraging predicament of Verdun.

Two alternatives were presented to you which caused dissension between you and your son. The Crown Prince wanted to retreat to the lines we were holding before the offensive began, but you wanted us to advance a hundred yards up the plain so that the French could no longer look down into our shell holes and bombard us at will.

The Crown Prince had his reasons. He feared he would be recorded in history as the "smiling assassin of Verdun," the name the French had given him. He knew that an advance such as you desired could only result in new hecatombs of dead, and shatter his last measure of prestige with the German soldiers.

Your Majesty also had reasons. In accordance with the counsel of the Chief of Staff, you considered a retreat an admission to the French that Verdun could not be captured, and to the German people that your promises had no substance. This, you knew, might prove disastrous to your throne.

According to the French report, two weighty promises were made last February when you stayed at your son's headquarters to honor the launching of the offensive with your presence. You announced to us: "This will be your last offensive." And the Crown Prince announced: "Children, on the parade grounds of Verdun, His Majesty, your Emperor and King, will dictate the peace treaty to the French."

It is said you made other promises: to the army, that it would repeat the glory of Frederick the Great and that Verdun would outshine Waterloo, Sedan, and Tannenberg; to the industrialists, that Germany would not return to France and Belgium the industrial and mining regions it occupied; and to the German masses, "I will lead you into a glorious epoch!"

Thus, the French said, you became a victim of your own promises. You could not retreat from Verdun without jeopardizing your dynasty. You fought with a delaying action in the hope that there would be a *deus ex machina* in the form of dissension among the Allies, or a peace proposal from the British, or a victory at the Russian front—a hope that some miracle would happen to confirm the historical good fortune of the House of Hohenzollern.

The French report concludes with a question: "How many lives is the Hohenzollern Dynasty worth to the Kaiser, who, to save face, will not retreat from Verdun?"

It is this question which spurs me to remember my vow at Verdun, which plagues me more than the lice, the dysentery, and the hunger I feel while lying on the straw in the sick tent, with comrades dying to the right and left of me.

It is this question which drives me to write this letter, hoping to redeem for myself that which I pawned to God on the battlefield.

Permit me to rise now in spirit and pass through the barbed wire of the camp, through the French lines, to draw you out of the isolated, palatial setting of the Court, and to lead you into military reality. Allow me to escort you to the shell holes between Fleury and Fort Souville where I, your once eager volunteer, lay with the 67th Regiment, so you can see the flesh of your men mingled with the soil. This place we called "the Death Mill of Verdun." You would also see how untenable our position was. The French, securely entrenched in the plain rising above us, could observe our slightest movement. At the first ray of dawn, our machine gunner peeked over the rim of the shell hole in which we were barely settled, and was instantly shot through the center of the forehead. While the French machine guns were sighted upon each shell hole, the French 75s were laying an iron net over our heads. The heavy shells, like big black birds, seared the air. As if this were not enough, our own artillery, at times falling short of the mark, exploded in our midst.

I would ask you to call a roll of the dead from the nine-month offensive at Verdun. It would raise up French and Germans on a battlefield so small you could encompass it with the naked eye from the crest of Douaumont—so small the dead would have to stand on one another to find room. In those nine months at Verdun, more men fell than marched in Napoleon's Grande Armée to Russia.

EPILOGUE

In the roll call, you would meet those men from our company. One would say, "My name is Berend; I was born in Berlin, I am forty-two years old, a butcher, and the father of five children." A second would say, "My name is Holsten; I was born in Danzig, I am twenty-eight, and I am a bookkeeper." A third would answer, "I am Schroeder; from Cologne, a volunteer and twenty years old. I studied medicine. I lost two brothers at the battle of Langemarck." Each would end his story with the words "I died for *Kaiser und Reich*." . . .

I would lead you along the same road, across the Meuse, to Verdun, which we few survivors traversed eighteen days ago. You would see, as we did then, a cathedral on the hill towering above the smoke and fire from the houses as if the city were elevating it, with its two spires pointing to the sky like two fingers in solemn oath: "We shall stand."

I would show you the square at the foot of the towers where General Herr, commander of the French fortress of Verdun, inspected us, the ragged remnants of your Fifth Army. Is this not the same "parade ground" where Your Majesty said you would inspect a beaten French army and dictate the terms of surrender? Your eyes would fall on the words of Joffre, Pétain, and Nivelle painted on the walls of the ruins surrounding us, reminding the French soldiers that their homeland was invaded and exhorting them to die on the spot rather than to yield. I read in the proclamations of your generals, Your Majesty, that we were fighting for *"Kaiser und Reich"* and that the "honor of Germany" was at stake.

I would then take you along the road I trudged to the prison camp. Passing the cemetery wall, you would see painted on the stones, in red blood, huge letters, "FIVE KILOMETERS TO THE SLAUGHTERHOUSE." And beneath it an arrow pointing to Verdun. What war-weary, cynical Frenchman could have painted this sign? As we prisoners plodded along this road, fittingly named La Voie Sacrée, because it was the only lifeline between Verdun and Paris, we passed regiment after regiment of Frenchmen, who cursed us, "*Sale boche! Kaiser kaputt!*"

I would lead you on to Souilly and show you the place where

eighteen days ago we dragged ourselves through the streets and an old washerwoman forced herself between the ranks of our guards, spat at us, and screeched, "You have killed my son!" A comrade who limped beside me in our sad procession said, "I never thought I would be ashamed to be a German. I don't think I can survive this day. I will commit suicide." At that moment I felt pity for Your Majesty. What terrible guilt you must feel when, through the letters you receive from the mothers of the dead, you learn of the despair and misery the war has wrought.

I would conduct you to the steps of the city hall of the village where, at the beginning of your offensive, General Pétain stood watching the French soldiers march toward Verdun. Without hiding his tears, he asked his staff, "How many will return?"

Does Your Majesty now see what a terrible guilt I would feel if I did not speak out? I can no longer wait to fulfill my vow, for in this sick tent I do not know if I will live to see tomorrow. I can only serve God by serving mankind. Hence this outcry to you.

I implore Your Majesty to consider the losses that this war is costing the Kaiser and Reich. Allow me to testify that General Ludendorff was wrong when he announced, "The Germans at Verdun are fighting a battle of attrition which will eat into the flesh of the French infantry like a gnawing ulcer." What I have seen as a common soldier in the front line was indeed a battle of attrition, but for both sides. If the enemy is bleeding white, then we are, too.

What has become of me, Your Majesty's volunteer who, inspired by your speeches in 1914, could not join the army soon enough? How I dreamed of riding at your side through the Arc de Triomphe in Paris! Indeed, I marched through France, but not in triumph. I goosestepped on the cobbled streets of Verdun, but not before Your Majesty's generals—before the French. A young French lieutenant cried at us in Alsatian German: "Are you hungry? Sing 'Deutschland über Alles.' Are you thirsty? Sing 'Die Wacht am Rhein'; the Kaiser will come and save you." Reduced to a number in a green prison uniform, I was despised and smitten behind barbed wire before I could understand the protest made by Albert Einstein, the foremost mind in Berlin, against the 1914 Belgian invasion. His words "Force attracts only men of low morality" were passed over by Your Majesty's courtiers, who sneered, "Einstein is a moral leper."

The French say in their report that in not retreating from Verdun you only want to save face. I believe I express the opinion of many soldiers when I say that in this war it is not the Dynasty of Hohenzollern, it is not the honor of the Reich, which is at stake, but humanity. If our military statisticians gloat that in this or that battle the enemy lost twice as many men as we, they are blind to the fact that the same hate and the same agony of dying is released on both sides. These spiritual forces hovering over the battlefield will leave more black chapters in history and engender new wars.

With each day that the war drags on, how many of the young Frenchmen and Germans now marching will be added to the roll call of the dead? How many hopes and dreams will die on the battlefield with them? How many contributors to humanity will be lost?

If I were once again to hear the call of my country, I would respond; but this time I would realize that though the responsibility for my actions belongs to my superiors, the responsibility for my conscience is mine.

Your Majesty's volunteer,
Wilhelm Hermanns
Machine Gun Company
67th Regiment